RALPH NADER PRESENTS
MORE ACTION FOR A CHANGE

# RALPH NADER
PRESENTS

# MORE ACTION FOR A CHANGE

## Kelley Griffin

**DEMBNER BOOKS**

*New York*

**About the Author**

As a journalism student and news editor of the *Daily Cougar* at the University of Houston, Kelley Griffin handled campus and community issues. Since graduating, she has worked for Ralph Nader, Jack Anderson, the Telecommunications Research and Action Center, and the American Association of University Women, covering Congress, federal agencies, and business and consumer groups.

Ms. Griffin is now enrolled in the Masters of Journalism Program of the University of California at Berkeley.

Dembner Books
Published by Red Dembner Enterprises Corp.
80 Eighth Avenue, New York, N.Y. 10011
Distributed by W. W. Norton & Company, Inc.
500 Fifth Avenue, New York, N.Y. 10110

Copyright © 1987 by Ralph Nader.
All rights reserved.
No part of this book may be reproduced in any form without permission in writing from the publisher, except by a reviewer who wishes to quote brief passages in connection with a review written for inclusion in a magazine, newspaper, or broadcast.
Printed in the United States of America.

**Library of Congress Cataloging-in-Publication Data**

Griffin, Kelley.
  Ralph Nader presents more action for a change.

  Includes index.
  1. Political participation—United States. 2. Lobbying—United States. 3. Public interest—United States. 4. Nader, Ralph. 5. College students—United States—Political activity. I. Title.
JK1764.G75   1987        323'.042'0973        86-29138
ISBN 0-934878-62-5
ISBN 0-934878-63-3 (pbk.)

*To my parents, Don and Juanita Griffin*

"All the love we come to know in life springs from the love we knew as children."

—*Thomas J. Langley*

# Contents

|  |  |  |
|---|---|---|
| *Preface* | | *xi* |
| *Introduction by Ralph Nader* | | *xv* |
| 1. | Public Interest Research Groups Take Shape | 1 |
| 2. | Research and Beyond | 14 |
| | *Surveys and Reports • Watchdog Projects • There Oughta Be a Lawyer . . . • Lobbying for Social Change • U.S. PIRG* | |
| 3. | PIRGs in Action | 39 |
| | *Students Battle for a Bottle Bill • Helping Millworkers Breathe Easier • CALPIRG and the Meat Scandal • Truth in Testing • Voter Registration • Dealing with Lemons* | |
| 4. | PIRGs in Action: New York PIRG | 75 |
| | *Lobbying • Citizens Wake Up to the Toxic Nightmare • Banking on Citizen Action • Acid Rain • Property Tax* | |
| 5. | PIRGs in Action: Colorado PIRG | 110 |
| | *Hazardous Wastes • Renters' Rights • Challenges from the Right • Making It Happen* | |
| 6. | Student Activists/Public Citizens | 131 |
| | *Kenneth Ward • Jill Siegel • Bob Chlopak • Marjy Fisher • Jim Rokakis • Marsha Gomberg • Karim Ahmed* | |

| | | |
|---|---|---:|
| 7. | PIRGs: Action and Reaction | 176 |
| 8. | PIRGs: The Future | 193 |
| | Appendix A. How to Start a PIRG | 200 |
| | Appendix B. Directory of Public Interest Research Groups | 214 |
| | *Index* | *217* |

# Acknowledgments

I would like to gratefully acknowledge the support of my family, who provided me with very special, long-distance encouragement, and Ellen Hosmer, who shared her considerable editorial skills and many cups of coffee during the course of this project.

Many others contributed both editorial and moral support, including John Richard, whose insight helped guide the project from beginning to end; PIRG leaders including Walter Hang, Jon Motl, Kirk Weinert, Tom Novick, Donald Ross, Doug Phelps, and Tom Wathen, who offered their knowledgeable perspectives; Ron Brownstein, whose earlier reporting on PIRGs provided the groundwork for some sections; Kate Duffy, Tim Massad, John Fitzgerald, Martin Rogol, Louis Nemeth, and Jane Margolis, who also contributed ideas and time to this project; Anna Dembner, who lent a keen editorial eye; and several dear friends, who kept me light-hearted through the project's ups and downs. I am very thankful for all of their efforts.

Particular thanks must go to Ralph Nader for his dedication and faith in students, and to the countless students who have worked in Public Interest Research Groups to empower citizens and make society more just.

# Preface

As Ralph Nader predicted years ago, students have the commitment and talent necessary to bring about social change. What they needed, Nader said, was an organization that would channel that talent and commitment effectively. They now have the organization: Public Interest Research Groups, or PIRGs for short. Since 1970, when PIRGs were started on college campuses with the help of Nader and his associates, the common notions of student activism have been greatly expanded.

This book tells the story of public interest research groups and how they have been a vehicle for student participation in such arenas as the courtroom, the legislature, local government and federal agencies, and town squares. PIRGs are different from many student organizations in history because they are funded and run by students, who hire professionals—attorneys, scientists, researchers—to lend skill and continuity to their efforts. This book describes how PIRGs were started and the issues they tackle; it portrays the personalities and commitment of the students and full-time staff working for PIRGs. Through PIRGs, students have uncovered everything from auto repair rip-offs to deadly toxic chemicals in drinking water sources, from dangerous and banned children's toys being sold in department stores to the lack of planning for emergency evacuation of people living around nuclear power plants.

PIRGs also have lobbying programs through which students promote legislation by meeting with representatives and their staffs, testifying before committees, and organizing people in the community to support legislation. PIRG support for issues, ranging from environmental protection to reform of hearing aid sales practices, has resulted in useful and important laws being enacted. An important consequence of these efforts has been the training and involvement of a new generation of citizens before and long after their graduation.

In 1971, Ralph Nader and Donald Ross outlined the potential of public interest research groups in *Action for a Change*. But, even with PIRGs on 175 campuses in 25 states, and in Canada, no book has been written about how that potential has been realized. There is a clear need for a current book on PIRGs that describes how students have become pacesetters in community affairs. *More Action for a Change* was written for public officials, community leaders, teachers, members of other citizen action groups, and students who want to know the history, scope, and direction of contemporary student activism.

Not only does the book highlight the issues PIRGs have worked on, but it brings you in touch with the people—how their participation led to changes in their career plans and personal commitment to the public interest. For example, it tells of Jill Siegel, a nineteen-year-old who joined the New York PIRG Legislative Program and, after six months' work, saw a bill to protect consumers from fraud in hearing aid sales become law. A NYPIRG study had revealed that hearing aid dealers were selling their generally elderly customers hearing aids when, in many cases, they did not need the $300 devices. Other customers who actually needed further medical

*Preface*

attention were told the hearing aid would solve their hearing problem. In order to save customers thousands of dollars each year and ensure that their medical needs were met, NYPIRG proposed a bill that required a doctor's prescription be issued for anyone wishing to purchase a hearing aid. Siegel was new to the legislative process, but with guidance from NYPIRG's executive director, Donald Ross, she formed a coalition of audiologists, senior citizens, and advocacy groups for the hearing impaired, met with legislators and their staff, overcame intense pressure from the hearing aid industry, and pushed the bill right up to its passage the last day of the 1974 session. From that semester on, Siegel's career plans were different—she studied law and is now an attorney for a Bronx legal aid society.

The book also looks at Bob Chlopak, who started organizing a PIRG in Washington, D.C., as a college freshman. He later became head of the Political Action Committee for Friends of the Earth, a national environmental group, and has just been named director of the national Democratic Senate campaign committee. Chlopak says that not only did PIRG allow him to choose a profession, it also gave him the skills that he needed to be involved in the public interest movement. But, as the book shows, PIRGs are not just for undergraduates. Karim Ahmed was a thirty-two-year-old Ph.D. candidate in physics when he helped organize the Minnesota PIRG in 1971. He spent the next two years juggling his time between his wife and two children, the PIRG, and the laboratory. And he learned that he wanted to apply his science background to the public interest movement. Today he is head of the science branch of the Natural Resources Defense Council.

Many people reading the book, whether they are students or nonstudents, may be surprised to learn a law they have taken advantage of, such as the "lemon law" that makes it easier for the owner of a defective auto to seek compensation, was passed because of the efforts of PIRGs. Even if they are familiar with some of the work of the PIRGs, they will find a wide range of PIRG activity that they may not have known about. Readers can also gain insights into how the combination of community organizing, lobbying, and research can bring about change and enrich the courses students take at the same time.

With the PIRG movement entering its eighteenth year, the book provides the public with the first in-depth chronicle of these unique student groups—groups that will serve a vital function in communities for years to come.

K. G.

# Introduction

The student movement of the 1960s showed that students have the potential for providing the direction, personpower, and ideals to have an impact on society. Young people of that era were concerned with problems that tended to be visible and readily susceptible to direct action—the Vietnam War was raging and blatant racial discrimination was under challenge. In the 1960s and early 1970s, in part due to student protests, policy makers changed positions on both the war and civil rights. But newspaper and television commentators viewed the student movement as dead or dying—"Gone is the movement of the 1960s," they would tell us with a touch of sadness or glee, depending on their politics. Sit-ins are out, toga parties are in—or so the media said.

While the media highlighted one student fad or another, some major interests persisted. Students were still concerned about the quality of life around them, and many were still doing something about it. They were not as demonstrative as their counterparts in the sixties, but their ability to be effective was undiminished. The complex issues of the 1970s demanded more diverse approaches than the direct protests typical of the sixties. The draft was gone, the Vietnam War was scaled down, and civil rights legislation had been passed. Many abuses were perceived as less obvious, and knowledge of law, economics, science, and engineering were frequently required to uncover problems and propose solutions.

As activists spoke on campuses, they began to observe that students wanted to do "good works" but lacked the organizational structure to translate idealism into longer-term constructive action. From the outset, students were attracted to the public interest research group (PIRG) model. First organized seventeen years ago, PIRGs now operate in twenty-five states and Canada. PIRGs are student-run, student-funded nonpartisan organizations that conduct research, advocacy, organizing, lobbying, and educational and media campaigns on a wide range of issues such as consumer rights, social justice, environmental protection, political reform, energy policy, and government responsibility. PIRGs were formed to convince students and other consumers that "you can fight City Hall!"

PIRGs provide student growth and education through direct experience that will develop both a commitment to a lifetime of citizen action and the skills necessary to be effective as activists. PIRGs also act as a counterforce to the organized economic and political power that can abuse American society. PIRGs represent the underrepresented—the broader "public interest"—as opposed to the many powerful and well-represented private or special interests.

These objectives are fulfilled primarily through research and education; students document a particular social problem and then attempt to marshall public opinion behind efforts to achieve reform.

PIRG reforms are seen as a means of improving society under our framework of constitutional rights and through society's major institutions. PIRGs work within the rules of the system—and with society's major institutions. As a result, many PIRG projects benefit from

*Introduction*

cooperation with policy makers at the local, state, and federal levels.

In a PIRG, the student board of directors, elected by their fellow students, hire professional organizers, researchers, and lobbyists to support their efforts and to provide continuity and a permanent base to the PIRG's work. At every juncture, however, students have the opportunity to learn by doing. Students not only select the projects PIRGs work on, they also determine the tactics and strategies that will be used. They combine knowledge with action in working on PIRG projects; the experience and skills they gain are invaluable assets for whatever they choose to do in the future, and can even earn them academic credits. Because of the structure and organization of PIRGs, three unique features have become the legacy of the movement: longevity, constant renewal as an institution, and proof that scholarship by students should be taken seriously.

The one underlying principle behind all PIRGs is that students are citizens, and that therefore their education should include experience in recognizing and solving society's shortfalls. Beyond that basic premise of students as citizens, PIRGs do not cling to any dogmatic ideology; they are simply democratic in operation and philosophy. College or university students vote democratically to form a PIRG on campus and to tax themselves to support it, student members then democratically elect PIRG leaders, and those leaders democratically choose the issues the PIRG will work on. The goal of PIRGs, then, is to give students and others the information and skills needed to function effectively in a democratic society—a goal that is often overlooked by high schools, colleges, and universities.

In PIRGs, students plan, implement, and follow up on sophisticated projects. These projects can be two-day surveys that call attention to a problem, or books that take two years to complete. After the research is done, students get the word out to the public and to appropriate officials or lawmakers. In addition to the usual publicity and media channels, several PIRGs use campus radio station facilities to produce syndicated radio shows on issues of student and community interest; others, like CALPIRG in San Diego, have had their own cable TV shows. Because of the volume of material they produce, some PIRGs have their own printing and graphics equipment for creating brochures, flyers, booklets, reports, and posters. Most PIRGs produce regular newsletters that go to students, community people, news media, and elected officials.

Most PIRGs offer some kind of hotline or action centers, with assistance on everything from consumer complaints to income and property tax matters. Sometimes the problems under study require legislative solutions. Here the prior PIRG work on an issue is invaluable; the most effective PIRG advocates (often student interns, supervised by a staff lawyer) approach their work as lobbyists armed with extensive research on a problem, backed up with real-life stories or experience gained through an on-going action center. In this way, PIRGs have successfully defended product liability laws and obtained improvements in small claims systems, better regulation of auto-repair shops, stronger protection for the elderly against fraud, and fairer property tax laws, among many others.

Part of successful advocacy is being able to demonstrate to politicians that there is a powerful constituency behind a certain proposal. Since PIRGs are based on the notion that students belong to the larger community, not just to the campus, it is natural that PIRGs reach out to the community to build up support for their initiatives.

PIRG community organizing takes on many forms. Sometimes simple petition-gathering or letter-writing drives grow out of a consumer action center or out of a

## Introduction

PIRG-sponsored radio show. Other times, well-planned, multistaged campaigns involve door-to-door leafletting, rallies, and community meetings. PIRGs with established door-to-door outreach programs have access to a network of tens of thousands of citizens who can be called on to do intensive grass-roots lobbying when necessary (an approach that worked well for the Massachusetts PIRG during the victorious 1981 fight to pass the state's bottle bill). Other PIRGs have done community organizing among low-income people—the New York PIRG in low- or moderate-income urban communities, for instance, and New Mexico and California PIRGs among Chicano farm workers.

Sometimes the courts are the best forum for addressing problems. PIRG lawyers have sued successfully in a number of instances—to stop improper expenditures of government funds, to protect constitutional rights, and to prevent government or private action that would endanger the environment, among others.

PIRGs also intervene in regulatory hearings—for instance, by representing residential consumers in utility rate-setting proceedings, or fighting environmentally unsound proposals.

Today there are more than 350 professional staff people employed by the PIRGs to help them carry on their work.

Over the past seventeen years students have been building a movement by combining solid research with organized action. Indeed PIRGs have accomplishments that are as diverse as they are impressive:

- Massachusetts PIRG published the report "Hazardous Waste in Our Drinking Water" in April 1986 and successfully obtained voter passage of the Hazardous Waste Cleanup Initiative in November 1986 after collecting one hundred

twenty-nine thousand petition signatures to place the measure on the ballot.
- Legislation written by MOPIRG, signed into law in early May 1986, will force at least 70 percent of Missouri's banks to shorten their check-clearing periods.
- Ontario PIRG and New York PIRG sponsored an educational "acid rain caravan" in New England and Canada in the summer of 1982.
- Several PIRGs joined in a nationwide student effort in 1982 to oppose federal budget cuts in financial aid for higher education.
- Minnesota PIRG litigated successfully in 1982 to gain major energy-conservation and antipollution-program concessions from a utility applying to construct a new coal-fired power plant north of Minneapolis.
- New York PIRG advocated successfully in 1979 for the nation's first truth-in-testing law regarding multiple-choice standardized testing.
- A California PIRG inquiry into fraudulent beef grading and price fixing was featured on a *60 Minutes* report in 1977, and led to fairer beef retailing practices in San Diego grocery chains.
- Vermont PIRG won legislation in 1973 establishing the country's first public dental health program for children.
- Indiana PIRG has conducted the country's longest-running grocery price survey, since 1972.
- New Jersey PIRG has sponsored the very successful "streamwalkers project," which monitors water pollution and industrial discharges in New Jersey; New York PIRG has produced several major reports on toxic chemical contamination in

*Introduction*

New York State, and its work has been featured on two *60 Minutes* reports.

In addition, PIRGs have worked to eliminate discrimination against students by auto insurance companies and banks; they have established food cooperatives, consumer hotlines, and small-claims-court advisory services, and they have published a variety of useful reports—such as New Jersey PIRG's manual on solar energy and others on financial aid, property tax, banking services, toxic wastes, and auto repair.

A national PIRG movement is active and growing. The state PIRGs have established a national office, which helps students to organize new PIRGs and provides support services to the individual state PIRGs. Organizing drives to establish new PIRGs are continuing across the country.

The PIRG movement has been endorsed by national leaders over the years. In a special message in 1978, President Carter called on "faculty, university administrators, and all concerned students . . . to provide the support necessary to PIRGs so they may further expand their valuable work in solving some of the pressing political and social problems of our country."

Despite all that PIRGs have done they still face some obstacles. Though there are still plenty of serious problems today to be worked on by PIRGs, it is more difficult to link the idealism of students to the more complex and more diffuse problems of today. We are faced with a seller-sovereign economy that includes sellers who are monopolistic or oligopolistic. Less ethical business executives use significant resources trying to persuade consumers to buy what the sellers want to sell, notwithstanding the availability of more efficient, safe, economical, durable, and effective alternatives. This economy results in widespread price-fixed products and services; product fixing to thwart innovation; deceptive packaging and false advertisements;

wholly ineffective or hazardous drugs; product obsolescence; energy-wasting vehicles, appliances, and other products; unsafely designed cars; junk food; serious product side effects such as pollution and poor land use; adulterated products; overselling of credit, insurance, and alleged health care—all complex problems to solve. We are reaching the point where the more default there is by citizens toward major pressing problems, the bigger the penalty. Fifty years ago if citizens did not do much about their electric utility, they paid a few dollars more on their monthly bill. Now if we do not do something we end up with a nuclear plant a few miles away and trucks and railway cars carrying radioactive waste. Different responses, and different consequences, result from citizen inactivity or indifference. Whether it is the arms race, asbestos, pesticide contamination, or acid rain and the greenhouse effect of carbon dioxide build up, there is an inescapable impact on the quality of community life. Now, because of the interdependence of society and the velocity of technology's impact, many perils know fewer boundaries.

The biggest immediate hurdle, however, is that most students do not adequately know the historic role of earlier students in American history and their contemporary role. First of all, they do not look at themselves enough as a unique class. In the United States there are thirteen million college students: community college, undergraduate, and graduate.

Students who are thirteen-million strong do not even have one weekly national television program that addresses what they are doing and thinking about outside the athletic arena. There is little self-realization that students need, deserve, and can demand such a program because they do not look at themselves as a class in the population, engaged in very interesting activities on campus. There are engineering students who are further

*Introduction*

developing solar energy and new kinds of automotive engines. Students are artists, poets, activists. They deserve the kind of attention now paid to the foolishness and the rites of spring that get most of the publicity.

Second, students underestimate their own power. If intimidated by university trustees who deny their democratic or educational rights, they must look for ways to challenge the trustees, uncover their conflicts of interest, and appeal for alumni and community support. They should realize that they can become the statewide experts on an issue, and that collectively they can put together a successful information or legislative campaign. It takes time, planning, and skill, but it can be done. Some people forget that students have been key organizers or backers of the major American social movements of the past two decades: the civil rights movement, the antiwar movement, the cultural movements of the 1960s, the women's movement, the welfare rights movement, and the environmental and antinuclear movements. And still today they have the time, energy, idealism, and resources at their disposal to act on the movements of today and the future.

Students today do not lack the basic generic idealism or desire for a better society. They do not lack the analytical ability to get the facts and the truth out about issues. Indeed, they can use the experience of past students' movements to build upon. But absent are street demonstrations, the draft, a disdained war, and other provocations and motivations that stir the young to action; instead, students face larger debts and a tighter job market than in the sixties. Nevertheless, in essence students are the same today as they were in the 1950s, the 1960s, and the 1970s.

So students need to look at their present assets. Students today are in different ways as important a source for citizen action as workers, homemakers, retired people, farmers, or other such groups of people in the United

States. As a class, they measure up quite well both in terms of visibility and impact.

Students have four important assets that always should be remembered. They are near the peak of their idealism. They have access to technical information that is highly desirable in any kind of public policy struggle, to libraries, laboratories, and faculty.

Third, students can double-track their scholarly or academic work with their civic action. For instance, in political science courses, students can profile members of Congress or agency heads and disseminate what they learn through the media. In chemistry and biology courses, students can test drinking water, air samples, and food contamination and apply the knowledge to action.

A steel worker is going to have trouble going to the steel mill, putting in a day's work, and fighting pollution at the same time. The worker might be fired for being an advocate. Students are much freer, which is another asset. They are at an age and in a situation more conducive to assuming bold steps, to going out to protest and to demonstrate. The invisible chains are not so tight.

Fourth, students have their own media—newspapers and radio stations—and their gathering halls in which to meet and rally for their causes. Most citizens do not have these ready facilities where they are every day. What remains to develop is a frame of reference and sound directions for student energies. Students need to compare their rights with the rights, for example, of peasants in dictatorships—who cannot speak out, cannot protest, cannot demand better working conditions, cannot stop police brutality, cannot have democratic elections. The peasants feel they do not count, and they are alienated and they are blocked from participating in their own society.

The United States is different from many other nations because, in a thousand little ways over two hundred years, enough few people have at crucial times

*Introduction*

reversed the slide toward authoritarianism and brutality and cruelty. Today, students in other countries are on the ramparts risking their lives to get a fraction of the rights students in the United States have and do not use.

In our schools and universities, there is inadequate emphasis on learning the civic skills needed to study, evaluate, and improve society. Students are not encouraged to develop citizen skills. This results in a shameful waste of human potential and in millions of students who lack civic self-confidence. Given the opportunity, many students could become effective advocates for democratic solutions to our society's problems.

Our educational institutions are in large part neglecting an important mission. Students rarely have the opportunity to study the phenomenon known as corporate crime even though it is widespread in the United States. Engineering or physics courses do not provide students with an opportunity to apply what they have learned to a particular issue in the community that invites the merging of theory and practice. A pollution exposure or a sewage-system problem could provide a clinical opportunity for students to contribute to their community.

Students are citizens, they are buyers, they are or will be taxpayers—yet they are not taught enough about the ways citizenship skills can improve their performance in these roles.

Most students do not know how to shop wisely for credit, insurance, or a car. In the aggregate, this means that we will continue to have a seller-sovereign economy, not a consumer-sovereign economy.

Many students are not involved in civic activity because they have too many personal anxieties and concerns and problems. Different commitments and different priorities for more important civic purposes such as environmental health, a just government, or minority rights can help dissolve or reduce these personal perplexities.

Thousands of students have found it quite fulfilling to work with their own student public interest research groups. Students can learn and grow and start to be judged by what they do—rather than by their looks or their socioeconomic status. PIRGs allow students to learn how to manage an organization, affect their surroundings, and make their society a better one in which to live.

PIRGs are fine adjuncts to classroom education because practical civic education meshes well with the humanities, social sciences, and physical sciences. Students never forget PIRG experiences. They know that they can be effective citizens. They know how to take on the legislature. They know how to prod a mayor, run referenda, build coalitions, get their views across to the public.

The role of a citizen, the role of an advocate, the role of a consumer are rarely evaluated. These evaluations are relevant to the pain and pleasure of students. These roles are intellectually stimulating and challenging—and necessary. We cannot simply inherit what we inherit and ride along like a toboggan sliding down a slope. We have got to carve out new paths. The hard fact is that each of us is both a private citizen and a public citizen. Most students want a good station in life, a good income, a home, a car, and a vacation cottage. That's being a private citizen. Usually people are adequately motivated in that area. What we need is a special effort in the public citizen area. That effort can be endlessly rewarding. It is a pleasure for students to fulfill themselves by applying the principles of justice in a community in a democratic forum—complete with debate, dialogue, advocacy, assertion, and implementation. You lose some, you win some. You keep going. You create positive benefits out of losing and adversity by becoming more strategically astute and more determined.

The commonly accepted definitions of worthy and remunerative work in any society need periodic expansion. In a nation characterized by a progression of humane

*Introduction*

values, what starts out as a sensitive effort by a few volunteers often matures into more deeply rooted structures defending and implementing these values on a daily basis. Fire fighting, libraries, soil conservation programs, women's right to vote, worker safety, civil rights, consumer rights, legal services for the poor, feeding programs for the hungry, laws protecting the many against the few, educational institutions and services—these are a small sample of social improvements stimulated into being by people who had a broader definition of human values or citizen work than their contemporary cultures recognized.

Today, as our society comes under even greater pressures and risks, people should have the opportunity to raise their sights and expand their horizons well beyond the vocational training that comprises so much of what is called their formal education. They should see that there are careers whose essence includes the right, if not the duty, to take their conscience to work every day. There are careers that encourage people to be primary human beings, not secondary persons who have to prostrate themselves before the imperatives of corporate or governmental managers in order to make a living.

Taking one's conscience to work opens more doors to the wedding of analytic skills and developed values for a better society. More creativity, initiative, and idealism result. Psychological satisfaction and other forms of job enrichment flow from such good works. Certainly the demand for such work is increasing. Citizens groups all over the country are redoubling their efforts to defend the fundamental rights of Americans and to strive for safe products, healthy environments and work places, civil liberties and civil rights. New civic efforts, on matters as disparate as the nuclear arms race and utility rates, are in need of a wide spread of talented people to consolidate their energies into permanent organization. Consumer-buying groups—from heating fuel to insurance—can use business administration and marketing skills along with suitable computer applications. The growing number of statewide citizen utility boards (CUBs)—which began in Wisconsin in 1979 when a state law required telephone, electric, and gas utilities to carry periodically in their monthly billing envelope a notice soliciting residential ratepayers to join the CUB—are in need of economists, mass-mailing specialists, organizers, engineers, and other skilled staff members. The expansion of telecommunications into cable, video, and other outlets does not have to be restricted to Madison Avenue definitions of content. A whole new set of people, values, and needs can find expression if the citizen-entrepreneurs are at work to help people know or find out more about their world.

With so much of our economy afflicted by trivial jobs chasing manipulated wants, with so many of our public institutions replete with dronelike sinecures, there are serious unmet needs—shelter, food, education, health, justice, peace, safety—that go begging for enduring, imaginative, and problem-solving attention. There are openings for people who want to work the frontiers of a just society, who want to be such a society's pioneers in foreseeing and forestalling abuses while inventing a future in pursuit of genuine happiness.

Nourishing the taproots of an ever deeper democratic society can be considered one of life's great joys. Fulfilling one's talents and dreams in such a quest is the antithesis of a job that, however well paying, makes you feel that you are just putting your time in, that life begins after the nine-to-five drudgery is over.

The wonderful aspect of social change work is the multiple exercise of your abilities that is involved. This work is not like the narrow-gauged responses on multiple-choice standardized tests. This work invites the application and development of multiple intelligences through the

*Introduction*

elaboration of one's mind, heart, and personality. No tunnel vision here.

The flow from knowledge to action draws upon the complete person with his or her catalytic and synergistic potential. Almost every skill and academic discipline can find a ready use in the complex drive for social change and in the protection and advancement of people and environmental rights in our society. Commitment, a reasonable self-confidence, a resiliency to overcome recurring adversities, a zest for work, and the ability to focus on larger goals without neglecting the daily details are some obvious traits of such a primordial advantage. A sense of humor for perspective and self-control also comes in handy.

And in good stead is an appreciation that there are not that many countries in the world where civic work can be carried forward as it can be in the United States under the blessing of our Constitution and the active citizens who give its words both foundation and life.

Many of America's students are among these active citizens. Thousands have joined together in public interest research groups, learning to combine their energy, academic knowledge, and organizational skills with their dedication to the community around them. They are preparing themselves for life and for work as citizen/activists—the true legacy of a democratic society.

This is their story.

Ralph Nader

O N E

# PIRGs Take Shape

"This country has more problems than it should tolerate and more solutions than it uses."* And among its unused solutions and resources are America's students—young citizens with the commitment and talent to bring about social change. What they lacked, until recently, was an organization that could channel their commitment and talent effectively. Now they have the organization—public interest research groups, organized campus by campus, state by state, all across the nation. PIRGs, as they are called for short, are student organized, student funded, and student run. Students establish each group, assess themselves to finance it, and, together with the professional staff that they hire, work on a wide variety of projects. They learn while doing, and in the process, they benefit their communities and America at large.

No one ever said organizing a public interest research group would be easy. Words like "creativity," "commitment," and "persistence" were used to describe the efforts it would require, but never "easy." After the organizing began to succeed and PIRGs gained funding, hired staff, put student volunteers to work, and completed projects,

*Quoted from *Action for a Change*, by Ralph Nader and Donald Ross (1972).

words such as "exciting" and "empowering" were commonly used, but still not the word "easy."

But then, doing important work is rarely easy. After more than a decade and a half of PIRG history, it is apparent that students are willing to work hard and long to achieve social change.

The precedent was set when the sixties opened and the relative calm of the previous decade dissolved as students played a large role in the drive for civil rights. The 1964 Civil Rights Act and successful voter registration drives were clear evidence that student actions could have an impact. Then, toward the end of the decade, an even more pressing issue came to a head, bringing a greater number of concerned citizens into the act.

Few Americans had passive attitudes about the war in Vietnam that was taking so many lives, particularly not those young Americans who knew they could become one of the grim statistics. Students were leaders in opposition to the war, with demonstrations and marches and sit-ins. The often extreme tactics were justified, in antiwar protesters' minds, when measured against the backdrop of extreme destruction caused by the war.

The seventies opened and the war was coming to a close, leaving in its wake hundreds of trained activists, and thousands more young people who could no longer ignore the problems facing society. And, as if from a newly opened Pandora's box, those problems were being revealed. People were taking notice of the nightmare of toxic pesticide pollution, detailed years before in Rachel Carson's book *Silent Spring*; of widespread poverty; of discrimination against women and minorities; and of unbridled corruption in government. Students began to look more critically at a society in which such problems could be so pervasive. Students were ready to confront the issues, but they lacked the organization needed to establish meaningful reform.

# PIRGs Take Shape

* * *

Enter, Ralph Nader. As one who had been seeking reform for years, Nader was eager to see students bring their energy to bear on critical issues. He believed a person was never too young to begin exercising the rights of citizenship. Nader's own history as a consumer advocate was a model for what citizens could accomplish. In a case often dubbed a David and Goliath story, Nader, as an individual citizen, became a persistent thorn in the side of General Motors and the auto industry in their unregulated collision course with motorist safety. Nader had become concerned about the number of traffic deaths, and with subsequent research he found that crashworthiness in automotive design was an almost nonexistent consideration for the automakers; concern for profits seemed to obscure the tens of thousands of people killed each year on the highways. As Nader continued looking into auto safety, he did free-lance articles on the issue for newspapers and magazines, and worked as a consultant and researcher to then Assistant Secretary of Labor Daniel P. Moynihan. In 1965, Ralph Nader's book *Unsafe at Any Speed* alerted America to practices in the auto industry that placed profit before what would prove to be simple, lifesaving design modifications. With his growing expertise, he was asked to become an advisor to Senator Abraham Ribicoff's Subcommittee on Executive Reorganization; Nader volunteered his time to help organize investigative hearings on auto safety. Nader's book was gaining national recognition and he was asked to appear on television and radio talk shows, and to testify in Ribicoff's second round of hearings on auto safety in February 1966.

All of this did not go unnoticed by General Motors, whose Corvair had been a focal point of Nader's book. This "lone crusader," as he was often referred to, had one of the largest corporations in the world very concerned. In

March 1966, it would be revealed in congressional hearings that GM was worried enough to hire a private detective to tail Nader and to question more than sixty of his friends, associates, and family, allegedly to determine whether he was involved in any litigation regarding the Corvair. Although GM President James Roche denied giving clearance for it, the detective's questioning, done under the ruse that Nader was being considered for an important job, often focused on Nader's personal life, not his legal work. Roche apologized to Nader before the Senate subcommittee.

But that was far from the end of the story. Nader was disturbed that a corporation could wield its power in this manner, so after lengthy consideration, he decided to sue for invasion of privacy. Any award, he announced at the outset, would be used to establish an organization to pursue auto safety issues and other consumer concerns. The legal battle lasted four years. In the end, documents had surfaced proving that GM had hired the detective to find whatever he could to discredit Nader, to "shut him up." As GM officials admit, and the investigation reports show, Nader's profile came out clean, but not GM's. In 1970, GM settled the case for $425,000, an amount thirty times greater than any court had ever awarded in an invasion of privacy case.

The money was used to establish a Public Interest Research Group in Washington, D.C. Nader hired a staff of twelve, including practicing lawyers and recently graduated law students, to examine a variety of issues ranging from the environment to pension reform. There was no lack of qualified people to work on public interest issues; more than seven hundred lawyers applied for the available positions. People working for Nader came to be called by a friendly press "Nader's Raiders" for their often scathing reports. The work at the PIRG, and at another Nader group called the Center for Study of Responsive Law, gave rise to an organization called Public Citizen, formed to monitor congressional activity on health and tax issues and to litigate.

While the work of these groups was bringing to light many of the abuses and negligence of the federal government, Nader knew that for every problem uncovered in Washington, there were thousands more in the communities across the United States. By now, Nader was regularly called on to give lectures on campuses nationwide, and he was consistently rated as one of the most admired people in America, even among often cynical students. In his speeches, Nader exhorted citizens to get involved and fight the problems locally that a growing number of people were fighting in the nation's capital. People were listening. And students, more than any other group, were set to follow his lead in public interest work. Nader saw that eagerness first-hand as he spoke with students in the United States and Canada, and when they began asking how they could be "Raiders" at their campuses and in their communities, Nader began answering, "Start a campus-based public interest research group."

Nader and two of his associates, Donald Ross and Jim Welch, went campus to campus encouraging students to direct their activism along this new path, tackling a wide range of issues. While past protests had served to draw the public's attention to some major issues, there were many other issues that needed more than attention: It would take laws to stop the pollution pouring out of many smokestacks and the industrial wastes being dumped into lakes and streams. Stronger regulations would need to be enacted to protect consumers from fraud and hazardous products. Unresponsive government agencies would only be called to task if there was clear documentation of their shortcomings. The kind of work Nader was challenging students to do would be more long-term than a rally or a march, yet would incorporate the same skills students had learned in their activism of the sixties. The demonstrations, he said, could be augmented by student research and advocacy of workable solutions to problems. In addition, he saw the campuses as fertile ground for training lifelong "public citizens," who would always play an important part in the decisions being made in society.

The issues the students would work on were significant, so it stood to reason that their organization would have to be sophisticated and powerful. But first, they would have to combat the problems that regularly plagued student movements—semester breaks, final exams, graduation. Nader had seen public interest work of his own require months and even years, and he knew the PIRGs had to be prepared for the long haul if they were going to be effective at prodding a government agency to action, or making citizens aware of their rights. A PIRG could not work to promote a bill in the legislature all semester, only to let it fail because it came up for a vote when most of the students had tough exams. Pressure on a company to stop polluting a river could not be allowed to abate because students who replaced graduating students did not know the issue; the company would not have much problem defeating such intermittent efforts.

It was in 1970, on the campus of the University of Oregon in Eugene, that Nader was finally able to garner support for the kind of student organization that could overcome these weaknesses.

Nader has always been a popular speaker on campuses, so it was not surprising when nearly half of the student body turned out for his speech. But despite the large and enthusiastic audience, Nader, Ross, and Welch did not truly anticipate the depth of the students' response and did not expect the idea of a student action group to get off the ground that day.

## PIRGs Take Shape

While Nader laid the groundwork that afternoon, he did not mention a hurriedly scheduled planning meeting set for that evening until his speech was over and the audience had already begun leaving the auditorium. To make matters worse, it was a Friday, and Ross remembers thinking that the evening's social events in Eugene would probably be a bigger draw than a last-minute meeting on social change. They had set the meeting for a room that held one hundred fifty people. They did not expect to fill it. They were wrong.

At least five hundred people showed up. Ross admits that he and Welch were a bit overwhelmed by the number, and they did not quite know where to begin. While Nader had been encouraging students to form such a group, he had not advanced a specific formula. That is where the commonly recognized student energy and creativity would come in. Ross points out, "Ralph had been making these proposals for years. He would tell students, 'Here are the things that need to be done, now you figure out how to do it.'" It was a fair proposition. At the meeting in Eugene, a unique organization took form. With professional staff people like Ross and Welch taking student ideas and providing direction, the concept of a new organization emerged—an organization that was student run, and student funded, and hired lawyers, scientists, organizers, and other professionals to make student action even more effective. It became the blueprint for public interest research groups on campuses in Oregon and across the country.

After the lecture and planning meeting, students formed organizing committees, publicized the idea, and gauged student support by circulating petitions. The support was overwhelming, and all seven schools in the state college system approved the establishment of the Oregon Student Public Interest Research Group (OS-PIRG). Several private schools and community colleges in the state followed suit. Administrators, who have final approval of whether any group can be established on campus, were not automatic supporters of OSPIRG. Donald Ross notes that since the Board of Regents heard not only from a small group of activists, but from students at the normally inactive campuses such as Eastern Oregon State and Oregon College of Education, it realized the support was widespread and approved the PIRG's formation.

Minnesota was the second state where students formed a PIRG. Ross remembers that, prior to the PIRG effort, the biggest petition drive at the University of Minnesota was against the war, and it collected ten thousand signatures. The PIRG organizers wanted to get twenty thousand on that campus. A core group of students got signatures from sixty percent of the student body of forty-two thousand in just two weeks, and by the end of the spring semester, more than fifty thousand students at schools throughout the state had signed on in support of the PIRG idea.

Petition drives are by no means easy, and certainly are not glamorous. They require talking to a lot of strangers, explaining the PIRG idea countless times each day and sometimes having to debate its worth with skeptics. Yet hundreds of thousands of signatures in favor of PIRGs have been gathered in that manner. The petition drive became an integral part of most organizing efforts. Not only did it allow organizers to talk with fellow students about the group, it also served as a measuring stick of support. With the majority of a campus population signing a petition in favor of PIRG, an official referendum could follow and students could vote to formally establish and fund a PIRG on their campus.

Just as the public was beginning to perceive the student movement as a fading phenomenon, the PIRG

## PIRGs Take Shape

idea began spreading from campus to campus. It was taking hold in so many places that, by 1973, columnist Jack Anderson wrote:

> Contrary to public impressions, idealism is not dead on campus. In visits to hundreds of schools and after looking over almost a thousand case histories of non-violent student activism, it is clear the spark glows and is even brightening a bit.
> A stronger, better organized movement is even more restlessly at work. It is called Public Interest Research Groups. Founded in 1970 by Ralph Nader, the groups now have operating budgets of well over $1 million, more than 500,000 members, and are on 135 campuses in 19 states.

The key to the success of PIRGs was to be their professional full-time staff. A student-run PIRG had to be flexible enough to meet the erratic schedule of students and shifting issues of the day, while having the resources to provide a base for consistent activism. That consistency was important; the group's credibility would rely on its ability to stick with an issue through several semesters, and even years, despite turnover among student volunteers. The staff of lawyers, scientists, and research directors would provide that consistency, and would guide the students through intricate projects, studies, litigation, community organizing, and lobbying.

And the key to that staff was an adequate and reliable source of funds.

Several funding methods have been adopted by PIRGs and college administrations since the students in Eugene, Oregon, petitioned to create the first PIRG chapter. But under each plan, PIRG fees have continued to be modest, ranging from $2 to $5 per term, and to reflect widespread student support.

The "refundable" fee is the most common method at private colleges, and it has been used at some public institutions. Under this system, the PIRG fee is included with other student fees, and the college administration gives the PIRG its per-student allotment after the semester begins. If students do not wish to support PIRG, they can obtain a refund directly from the PIRG.

In 1986, a federal appeals court with jurisdiction over New Jersey, Pennsylvania, and Delaware ruled against a unique version of the refundable fee system used by the New Jersey PIRG at the State University of Rutgers. The appeals court went out of its way to emphasize, however, that its decision did not apply to any part of the PIRG fee that was collected as part of the student activity fee, to "waivable" or other voluntary fees, or to fees of any kind at private schools. The U.S. Supreme Court refused to hear the case on appeal, thereby leaving each of the nation's other eleven courts of appeals free to reach its own conclusion on refundable PIRG fees.

In any case, most state schools elsewhere use the "waivable" fee, which is not affected by the decision. Under this system, the PIRG fee is also billed with other student fees, but students who do not wish to pay the fee can refuse or waive the PIRG fee by checking or initialing a box on either their registration form or their tuition bill.

Both of these funding systems are implemented by the college administration, which then passes the revenue on to PIRG. Some institutions (including the State University of New York) include the PIRG fee in the student activity fee, the funds from which are disbursed by student governments. The basic per-student per-term fee, however, is still utilized under this method. The student government allocation simply reflects the number of students registered.

So, while funding mechanisms vary, they each reflect the expressed desire of a majority of students to establish and fund a PIRG campus chapter at their college or university.

\* \* \*

## PIRGs Take Shape

In addition to being student funded, the professionally staffed PIRG was to be student run, and that aspect of the organization had to be developed as well. The structure had to ensure that students would have control of the organization, and that students and staff resources were used most effectively. Lengthy discussions resulted in a plan to have local and state boards of directors made up of students elected by their fellow students; the boards would guide the organization and the staff. After PIRGs in Minnesota and Oregon were organized with this plan, Nader and his staff of organizers wrote the book *Action for a Change*, which detailed the structure used by MPIRG and OSPIRG. The structure has been put in place by most PIRGs, with only minor changes and some additions to these basic functions:

- The local board mobilizes students and campus resources, organizes projects, elects members to the state board, and acts as a link between the campus and the state board, and between PIRG and other community and campus groups.
- The state board determines what issues are a priority for staff action, supervises the activity of local boards, and coordinates PIRG projects with other state or national public interest groups. In addition, the state board is responsible for hiring the executive director, who oversees the professional staff.
- The staff is charged with implementing the decisions of the state board, supervising student research, lobbying, and public education efforts; participating in those areas themselves; and handling financial and administrative details. These low-paying positions, requiring long hours, are not as difficult to fill as it might seem. Ross

explains that "there are very few jobs in our society that allow people to get paid for working on things they believe in completely. People will trade a nice office, regular hours, and hefty salaries to be able to do that kind of work." He admits those people may never be in the majority, but there seem to be enough to staff the growing public interest movement.

In determining the projects on which the group should work, the PIRG state board of directors looks at a number of factors: the importance of the issue and likelihood of its being affected by PIRG action; the amount of student involvement a project will offer; whether the PIRG's work would be duplicating rather than adding to the efforts of other groups; and whether, given the expenditures and amount of staff and student time an issue is likely to require, the outcome is worth PIRG resources. This assessment assures that student contributions and staff resources are used most efficiently, while allowing the group great flexibility in selecting its projects.

The Minnesota and Oregon PIRGs, frontrunners of the early days of public interest research groups, moved quickly into the realm of learning and doing. By 1972, both organizations had hired talented lawyers, scientists, writers, and researchers. Backed with a host of student interns, those PIRGs had already made their mark:

- A two-month study of Portland auto repair practices by OSPIRG students uncovered sufficient evidence of fraud and deception to initiate an investigation by the local district attorney's office and subsequent action against the offenders.

## PIRGs Take Shape

- MPIRG, in conjunction with local unions and the state AFL-CIO, conducted a major review of occupational safety and health laws and enforcement practices regarding asbestos in Minnesota. That report led to legislation banning the use of asbestos in new construction.
- MPIRG conducted a toy safety survey that alerted consumers to the perils of defective and hazardous toys. The report, which received national recognition, was one factor in the Food and Drug Administration's creation of a citizens' board to evaluate toy safety.

# TWO

# Research and Beyond

PIRG accomplishments in the early 1970s often served as models for other PIRGs and their first projects. Surveys of products and markets were tasks that newly formed PIRGs could start out with, allowing students to become familiar with techniques they would use later for bigger, more complex projects.

The technique that is basic to all work by public interest research groups is, as the name implies, research. Of course, students are familiar with course research—it usually means spending long hours in the library reading what others have written about a topic, and then trying to write about it in a new way. But researching for a PIRG project is different. It may mean compiling and comparing tenant laws, or it may mean interviewing people in the community or workplace to compile statistics on anything from consumer purchasing habits to job safety. PIRG researchers may go over voting records of legislators or monitor campaign contributions. Their inquiries range from gathering original data to slow and sometimes tedious surveying and interpretation of existing regulations and laws. What makes research for a PIRG project so different is that students know their thorough analysis of a problem will allow them to propose and work for solutions.

## SURVEYS AND REPORTS

The PIRG research that often gets the greatest public attention is the timely report that reveals an unjust pattern of activity by government or a widespread and dangerous way of doing business by a private party. One example is the 1976 study by PIRG in Michigan (PIRGIM) of the dangers of transportation of radioactive wastes from nuclear power plants where the wastes are generated to storage facilities miles away. The sixty-two-page report, *Fallout on the Freeway: The Hazards of Transporting Nuclear Wastes in Michigan*, was the first nongovernmental research on the problem. The report concluded that shipping radioactive wastes on the highways and railroads may be dangerous to nearby populations since the wastes can be released, either from faulty design or maintenance of the casks in which they are transported, or as a result of an accident.

PIRGIM's study and its recommendations were supported by articles and editorials in ten Michigan newspapers. It became the subject of national media attention, which resulted in more than four thousand requests for the report from the United States, Canada, Germany, and Japan. It inspired remedial state legislation providing for safety measures such as special training for the drivers of trucks carrying nuclear wastes and warning devices for the vehicles. The issues raised by the report were addressed by a number of communities that followed the Michigan example.

In 1974, '76, and '78, PIRGIM produced a series of equally important studies. The series, which was called *The Empty Pork Barrel: Unemployment and the Pentagon Budget*, used analytical techniques developed by a Yale University economist in 1970 to analyze the impact of military spending on major sections of the U.S. economy for the years 1968 and 1972. The reports concluded that, contrary to popular belief, the capital-intensive military industry was a poor creator of jobs per dollar spent. They concluded that the 1976 military budget of $80 billion would actually create 844,000 fewer jobs than might be created if the money were invested in civilian sectors of the economy. The study was important because it provided the first evidence to counter the widely held belief that the huge military budget was a fertile creator of jobs—an argument often used by legislators when they uncritically vote yes for huge Pentagon appropriations.

The Pork Barrel study was an example of work produced by a single staff member that brought acclaim to the whole organization. The then legislative director, Marion Anderson—who has gone on to head up her own research firm in Michigan, which looks at the impact of military spending and other government projects on various sectors of society—did most of the analytical work. She had a hunch that military spending did not create the number of jobs people generally assumed it did, but she went on to prove it, with her careful survey and the computer.

Again, the report was to reach beyond Michigan. Anderson testified before the U.S. Congress, and the study was covered in newspapers from Rhode Island to Oregon, cited by presidential candidates, reported in the nationally syndicated Jack Anderson column, and reprinted in the *Congressional Record*.

In Vermont, the success of VPIRG's first legislative effort stemmed from its report on the poor dental health of some thirty-five thousand children in the state's low-income families. The remedy proposed by the PIRG report, called *Nothing to Smile About: The Dental Health of*

*Research and Beyond*

*Vermont's Children*, was a "tooth fairy program," adopted by the legislature in 1973. The program, funded by general revenues, provides dental services for youngsters whose families cannot afford it.

When the PIRG in Maine began looking at evacuation plans for communities around a nuclear power plant, it was what the group did not find that made its report, *Hopelessly Hoping*, important to Maine residents. The Nuclear Regulatory Commission requires utilities with nuclear plants to submit evacuation plans for areas surrounding their plants in case of an accident. Yet, in 1975, Colby College student Josh Davis and Research Director Rob Burgess found that virtually none of the people charged with carrying out the evacuation plans knew what they entailed. Of course, that meant the average person in the small towns and countryside surrounding the plant had no idea what they would have to do in an emergency at the plant. What is more, the report showed that even if the plans, patterned after state-approved plans, had been widely disseminated, they still had shortcomings: The special sirens to warn citizens did not exist; no hospitals were prepared to handle radioactive contamination; the children at seven schools and numerous camps in the area had been completely forgotten—no evacuation plans at all had been made for them.

Newspaper accounts began to point out additional life-threatening twists to an evacuation. Maine's geography and weather combine to make for slow traveling on sharply curving coastline roads that are often veiled in fog. One newspaper described it this way:

> As sirens wail in the background, panicked citizens mob the roads, fleeing from imminent disaster. But the roads are clogged . . . evacuation comes to a standstill as a cloud of radioactive material settles over the countryside.

MORE ACTION FOR A CHANGE

What that scenario fails to consider, of course, is that there would not even be wailing sirens to warn citizens to flee. Except for the few people whom authorities could reach in person, many Maine residents would be caught unaware in the countryside as the radioactive material settled over it.

The Maine PIRG petitioned the state Public Utility Commission to require Central Maine Power Company to include complete and up-to-date evacuation instructions in the same envelopes as its customers' billing statements. The PIRG report and the news coverage it received were so effective that the power company agreed to comply with the request even before a ruling was made.

The title "research group" may seem to ignore all the other facets of PIRGs' work. But, in fact, all of their work is based on the accurate, extensive documentation of problems. It is from there that students can propose solutions, which is also an integral part of PIRG work. With this attention to resolving problems, students learn how to take those vital steps beyond discovery of unjust or dangerous situations. Just as students learn through a science laboratory about the functions of the human anatomy, society becomes a laboratory for students in PIRGs to understand the anatomy of government and business and the role of citizen involvement.

## WATCHDOG PROJECTS

In some cases, a PIRG will take on a watchdog project. It will monitor a situation to make sure existing regulations are being enforced and are serving their purpose. Often, this also entails educating the public about those regulations so other citizens can be monitoring them as well.

New Jersey is not a large state geographically, but it has

## Research and Beyond

the second largest concentration of chemical factories in the United States, and the third largest number—223—of known chemical waste dumps. Labeled a "chemical time bomb" by former New Jersey PIRG Director Ed Lloyd, the state has thousands of industrial plants discharging wastes into New Jersey's streams and lakes. NJPIRG students became "streamwalkers" in order to monitor discharge of pollution, and to report the conditions of waterways to the state and federal environmental protection agencies. They initiated the water projects soon after Congress enacted the Federal Water Pollution Control Act of 1972. To accomplish its objective, the act established the National Pollutant Discharge Elimination System (NPDES), which requires anyone discharging pollutants into the waters of the United States to obtain a permit. The permits specify the types and amounts of pollutants that may be discharged.

Equipped with hipboots, maps of streams, data sheets, and a list of industries and their discharge permits, students would hike or canoe along stream beds and make systematic assessments of sources of pollution. Their findings were written up in Stream Surveillance Reports, which were used by local community and environmental groups, as well as understaffed county, state, and federal agencies charged with monitoring industrial discharges. Not only did NJPIRG students keep track of whether industries were within limits of their permits, they also identified industrial dischargers that had not filed for permits, as required by law. By 1980, NJPIRG had more field inspection personnel walking the banks of rivers and streams than all of the state's public agencies combined. Not surprisingly, NJPIRG has found more violators than any other entity in New Jersey—in one county alone, the streamwalkers stopped more than twenty plants from discharging wastes without a permit. The program was so successful that the U.S. Environmental Protection Agency

(EPA) gave NJPIRG a grant to produce a how-to manual for would-be streamwalkers, and it gave former NJPIRG Director Ed Lloyd its Special Award of Merit for citizen environmental activism. The streamwalker program is still a part of New Jersey PIRG's effort to assure clean water for drinking, fishing, and recreation.

Several PIRGs, including those in North Carolina, Ontario, British Columbia, and Minnesota have been watchdogs of agencies charged with protecting workers' health. Few people realize that in 1973 alone, more than twice as many Americans died from job-related injuries or diseases than were killed in the entire Vietnam War. With that chilling statistic in mind, NCPIRG fought for stricter workplace standards to protect textile workers from brown lung disease, and Ontario PIRG issued an extensive *Workers' Guide to Health and Safety*. The guide describes workplace hazards and how to eliminate them, as well as how to apply for compensation from work-related illness or injury. As Patrick Reagan, then consultant to MPIRG and author of that group's worker handbook, said, "Present job safety legislation will never give adequate protection to workers unless the workers themselves exercise their rights to the fullest, unless they demand that the agencies set up to protect them function properly." Using PIRG handbooks as a guide, workers learn to do just that.

## THERE OUGHTA BE A LAWYER . . .

Many problems are called to a PIRG's attention by consumers who have been harmed or "ripped off" and who turn to PIRG for help. At least once in a lifetime, one feels a situation is unfair and may mutter, " There oughta be a law." Well, if a person happens to storm into a PIRG office with the same comment, it may be that a PIRG member will respond, "There is." What's more, the PIRG member can tell the disgruntled citizen, "We can give you information about the law, and if it is not being enforced, we have the resources to help see that it is."

Of course, PIRGs are not legal clinics with staff to take on individual cases, but when a situation represents "injustice for all," PIRGs are ready to go to court.

In a democratic system fraught with administrative and political pitfalls, it is often a PIRG attorney who ensures that the organization has access to a particular decision-making arena. PIRG lawyers provide important tactical flexibility for a PIRG, allowing it an alternative avenue for action when faced with a recalcitrant legislature, an unresponsive executive agency, or an irresponsible private sector.

PIRG attorneys perform a number of functions. These include drafting legislation and lobbying, writing and offering testimony, providing legal editing and advice for PIRG publications, and, of course, representing the PIRG in formal litigation in courts and agency hearing rooms.

Minnesota's PIRG, established in 1971, has had an active litigation program. It was the legal advice from leading Minneapolis attorney Allan Saeks (presently head of the Hennepen County Trial Lawyers Association) that helped develop a stable base for litigation work. Saeks also set up the MPIRG Foundation, which is funded by people in the community who want to support a student intern or a MPIRG project. In addition, MPIRG's first staff attorney left a large Minneapolis law firm—and took a cut in salary—to head the new PIRG program. With such support in its beginning stages, it is not surprising that MPIRG is one of the most active PIRGs on the legal front.

Over the last decade it has always employed at least two full-time litigators and has been a party in thirty-one court actions, filed amicus briefs in three actions, and intervened as a party plaintiff in four cases. In addition, MPIRG has been a party in thirteen administrative proceedings, including six petitions for agency rulemaking.

Amicus briefs, party plaintiff, and petitions for rulemaking may not mean much to the average student, which is precisely why a staff attorney is important to PIRG efforts. The student can see the problem, but may not know the legal recourse. That a PIRG has access to such recourse with its legal staff makes it harder for agencies or individuals to disregard a PIRG's work—they know it may mean going to court.

Some of MPIRG's lawsuits through the 1970s included a test case ensuring enforcement of the state's environmental rights act, several cases aimed at clarifying apparent "loopholes" in the state's tenants rights law, and the "police badge" case, where MPIRG sued the Minneapolis Police Department for allowing its helmeted (and unrecognizable) officers to remove their identification badges prior to using force to clear demonstrating students from streets near the University of Minnesota campus.

The 1970s also gave rise to MPIRG's most famous watchdog lawsuit. The case concerned the use of the National Environmental Policy Act (NEPA) to limit the cutting of virgin timber in the Boundary Waters Canoe Area (BWCA) in northern Minnesota.

The BWCA is now a congressionally protected, one-million-acre wilderness area that includes hundreds of pristine lakes and is a remnant of the once-great northern United States conifer forests. As the nation's sole "paddle-only" wilderness area, it had long been appreciated by hundreds of thousands of visitors including many Minnesota college students. Perhaps the most widely followed and popular issue among Minnesota students of the day, the preservation of the BWCA found constant support at MPIRG where students petitioned, lobbied, rallied, and,

## Research and Beyond

for seven years, assigned lawyers to defend the BWCA. The litigation began with a debate about whether the U.S. Forest Service could allow private companies to cut trees in the BWCA without first completing an environmental impact statement (EIS), as required by the newly passed NEPA. The EIS is an extensive study of how a proposed activity would affect wildlife, water quality, and the environment in general. The U.S. Forest Service did not believe it needed to do an EIS and refused to halt its timber sales.

MPIRG disagreed. In 1972 it filed its first BWCA lawsuit in federal district court and quickly won a temporary injunction banning the Forest Service from allowing logging, with its attendant road building, in the BWCA without first preparing an EIS. The temporary injunction was appealed by the Forest Service to the Eighth Circuit Court of Appeals, where the decision was upheld. The Forest Service quickly wrote an EIS that, perhaps not surprisingly, recommended timber cutting be allowed. Again MPIRG sued, this time alleging that the EIS was inadequate. Presenting expert witnesses, including a Forest Service scientist, MPIRG was able to prove there were deficiencies in the EIS, and the judge agreed. Again the Forest Service appealed. By now it was 1976 and this time the Eighth Circuit Court ruled in favor of the Forest Service. It was MPIRG's turn to appeal, and securing another temporary injunction while the appeal was in process, MPIRG requested a hearing before the U.S. Supreme Court. In late 1978 the appeal was denied and the injunction dissolved with that decision.

After six years of litigation, ten thousand pages of legal documents, the sustained efforts of three MPIRG lawyers, and six yearly changes in the MPIRG board of directors, the legal battle was over. While MPIRG lost the battle, it did not lose the war. During that six years of legal work, many of Minnesota's citizens had read and heard enough of the BWCA issue to take a stand. Polls consistently showed the public wanted the BWCA protected. A broad coalition of citizens groups, including MPIRG, had formed the Friends of the Boundary Waters Wilderness and by 1978 the group drafted and was supporting a bill in the U.S. Congress that would give permanent wilderness status (thus banning timber cutting) to the BWCA. The bill had great momentum, and even though the MPIRG injunction on cutting was lifted, private timber companies agreed to refrain from acting on their timber contracts until after Congress had a chance to act. The bill passed in mid-1979 and the BWCA—timber and roadless areas intact—stands for future generations as testimony to the value of consistent, long-term action by a public interest research group.

In addition to its government watchdog work, MPIRG attorneys also regularly challenge companies who engage in what MPIRG sees as unjust or unfair activities. These efforts have included several successful cases against General Motors because of "lemon" cars; a federal district court suit against the Minnesota Democratic and Republican parties asking that both parties be required to publicize the times, dates, and places of their precinct caucus meetings; a suit against the Minnegasco utility company for breaking and entering a customer's house; and a 1979 case against Ford Motor Company, claiming Ford should cover damages to a truck that were sustained when the owner was driving the vehicle "off-road" as shown in popular advertising of the truck. Introducing the television commercials as evidence, the case was decided in favor of MPIRG's client, a St. Cloud University student. Publicity from the decision, including a national wire-service story, caused Ford Motor Company to advertise its trucks more accurately.

\* \* \*

*Research and Beyond*

MPIRG, in a recent case, and also its first before the Supreme Court, challenged the constitutionality of the Solomon amendment, a law that forces draft registration-eligible students to sign an oath that they have registered before they will be eligible for federal financial aid. MPIRG decided to file a lawsuit on behalf of its members shortly after the law was passed. After almost two months of intensive research, MPIRG's senior attorney, E. Gail Suchman, and her researcher found four reasons why they believed the law was unconstitutional.

MPIRG believed the law amounted to a bill of attainder, which means Congress tries to determine guilt legislatively, and to punish without a trial. Bills of attainder were declared unconstitutional during the Civil War, when Congress tried to make doctors prove they had never treated any Confederate before they could get a license, and during the 1950s "red scare," when people were forced to prove they had not been associated with the Communist party before they could get government jobs. Along those lines, the Solomon amendment also would make students prove their "innocence" or be punished by not receiving financial aid.

The second point MPIRG made was that the amendment was a violation of students' Fifth Amendment right against self-incrimination, since those who refused to sign the oath would be considered guilty of not registering.

The third point was that the amendment denied equal protection under the law because wealthy students who do not need financial aid for their education would never have to sign such a document. Low-income students, who rely on financial aid, are disproportionately minorities and as a group are greatly affected by this law. In addition, because only men between ages eighteen and twenty-one are required to sign the oath, MPIRG argued that it also caused age and sex discrimination. MPIRG's fourth point was that the rule violates the privacy act of 1974.

After MPIRG first filed on behalf of its members, in November 1982, the district court judge would not give the group "standing" to the file suit because, he said, the case was not germane to MPIRG's work. Suchman says that ruling was "absurd. We represent students and this is a student issue." MPIRG appealed that ruling, but rather than wait until the appeal was heard, the group refiled on behalf of three students who had not registered and who were seeking financial aid. By March 9, 1983, Judge Alsop had issued a preliminary injunction to prevent the amendment from going into effect; on June 16 he issued a permanent injunction with a statement that, based on MPIRG's first two points, the amendment was unconstitutional. The Justice Department asked for a stay of the injunction pending appeal, but Alsop denied it. The government then went to the Supreme Court, where it received a temporary stay of the injunction until the high court decided the case.

Several colleges and universities filed "friend of the court" briefs in support of MPIRG, including the University of Minnesota, Swarthmore and Macalester colleges, Harvard University, and MIT. The Minnesota Civil Liberties Union became a party to the case two months after MPIRG filed it. *The Minnesota Daily*, a newspaper for the University of Minnesota that also serves the community with a readership of seventy thousand, wrote several editorials in favor of MPIRG on this case, and city newspapers in St. Paul and Minneapolis endorsed MPIRG's stance as well.

When the decision finally came, it was not in MPIRG's favor. The U.S. Supreme Court ruled in the spring of 1984 that the Justice Department could legally prevent students from receiving federal financial aid if they do not register for the draft.

MPIRG's former senior attorney James Miller says, "Lawsuits are important for policy and information reasons. They force decision-makers or business executives to confront their actions. They can't hide anymore once a lawsuit is filed, and in any case, the whole issue is covered in the press." With this thought in mind, Miller believes that even lawsuits that lose on procedural grounds bring about change because the propriety of the situation, regardless of its legality, becomes widely debated among people in the community.

Another area in which PIRGs are often involved is utility rate proceedings before state utilities commissions. Some states have a Public Counsel to represent citizens before the utilities commission. But that may not be enough. Utilities always have large legal staffs at work justifying increases, and public counsels may not have the staff and resources they need to make a strong case for denying the rate hike. What's more, since public counsels are generally appointed by the governor, they may have to be more concerned with politics than with consumers. That is why many PIRGs intervene before the public utilities commissions on electric, gas, and telephone issues. The Michigan PIRG has successfully argued before the Michigan Public Service Commission for the initiation of innovative rate structure changes designed to promote energy conservation, equalize rate costs between high- and low-volume users, and lower overall rates.

And a recent victory of Missouri PIRG further illustrates how PIRGs can help save consumers millions of dollars. Union Electric (UE), based in St. Louis, determined in 1981 that it would not need to build a planned second unit of the Callaway nuclear project because energy use in the state was not as high as expected. Yet, the utility wanted to pass on the cost of canceling the plant, approximately $84 million, to its eight hundred thousand customers by adding it to their electric bill over a five-year period. But in a 1976 referendum, which MOPIRG helped placed on the ballot, Missouri voters had said utilities could not charge for the cost of construction work in progress, or for the maintenance of land or equipment scheduled for use in a plant, before the plant supplies electricity.

UE argued that since the referendum said customers would not pay "before" the plant supplied energy, it does not address the issue of canceled plants that will never produce. MOPIRG and the Office of Public Counsel argued that voters intended to protect themselves from bearing the financial risk of constructing a power plant, whether the plant would eventually produce power or not. The public service commission agreed with the PIRG and the public counsel.

UE appealed the commission's decision to refuse to allow the utility to pass along costs of the canceled nuclear plant to consumers. In March of 1986, the court ruled that UE could not recoup the costs of the plant from consumers. While UE is likely to appeal again, the unanimous decision gives MOPIRG a strong case in higher courts.

Rich McClintock, executive director of MOPIRG, called the decision a "tremendous victory for the eight hundred thousand utility consumers in Missouri," who will each save approximately $100 as a result of this decision, and will be protected from having to pay for plants that will never provide them with power.

## LOBBYING FOR SOCIAL CHANGE

But what if there is not a law? Most PIRGs have well-developed lobbying programs that can promote legislation to fill in the gap of consumer protection. Once a PIRG's research identifies a particular problem the PIRG will often turn to its state legislature for action. As Donald Ross explains it, "Public education changes attitudes; the courts can strike down bad laws and occasionally make new ones.

*Research and Beyond*

But only the legislature exists to create new laws, and those new laws, properly enforced, can bring about social change."

While the lobbying programs help establish good laws, they also give students an extensive, hands-on course in government, one that cannot be matched in even the most vigorous college class. Students learn that elected representatives need not be beyond the rein of accountability of voters. They realize that not only do they have a stake in the lawmaking process, they also have the ability to affect that process.

As might be expected, action aimed at achieving the passage of a new law is more difficult than identifying the need for the law in a research report. A successful advocacy effort can often span several years and include coordinated, sophisticated action by many people. A proposal must be backed with extensive research to be presented to legislators, their aides, and the staff of legislative committees. PIRG lobbyists follow bills through the entire legislative process, including hearings, mark up, and final votes. Their sound evidence, viable solutions, and persistence have assured that the voice of citizens not represented by special interest lobbyists is heard. As former long-time Missouri PIRG Director Tom Ryan points out, "A PIRG presence in the state capitol is the best watchdog a democracy can have."

The issues around which PIRGs choose to formulate legislation usually spring from the interests of the state residents. For example, the proliferation of nuclear power plants and their attendant dangers had long troubled many Vermont residents. In response to this concern, the Vermont PIRG decided in 1974 to lobby for a bill, written by VPIRG, that would give the Vermont legislature final approval for the construction of any new nuclear power plants in the state.

The nuclear industry strongly opposed the measure.

The utilities claimed that by the mid-1980s additional power would be needed and it should be nuclear power. In an attack on democratic accountability, utilities argued that the legislature should not have a role in deciding about nuclear plant construction despite possible dangers the plants would present to Vermonters.

VPIRG and other citizen groups testified before the state's House Natural Resources Committee that there were safer choices to fill future energy needs. Dr. Allan Hoffman, a professor of physics and astronomy at the University of Massachusetts, criticized the utilities for not spending adequate time or money looking into alternatives other than nuclear power. He cited environmental damages that would be caused by nuclear energy generation and declared, "Rapid development of solar energy and other alternative technologies would result in a far safer world."

Despite the immediate need for the bill, the chairperson of the committee, Royal B. Cutts, announced after the hearing that he would pocket the bill, thereby blocking it during the 1974 legislative session.

But VPIRG was prepared to push the bill again in the 1975 legislative session. Once again at hearings, utilities touted the economic benefits of nuclear power, while VPIRG chronicled the opposition to it from the communities. Pronuclear lobbyists pursued a variety of delaying ploys. Meanwhile, in town meetings throughout the state, the public expressed sharp hostility toward utility rate increases and pronuclear lobbying tactics.

Under pressure from both sides, the House Natural Resources Committee compromised on a "negative option" clause. Under this plan, a proposed nuclear power plant would not need the legislature's approval, but would be subject to a veto by the legislature. Fortunately, by the time the bill was bandied about in another committee and was sent to the House floor, it once again contained the original provision that no nuclear power plant construction could start without majority approval of the state legislature. Finally, the House passed the bill, and after facing similar debate in the Senate Energy Committee, it was sent to the Senate floor and passed, 22–0. The governor signed it into law.

VPIRG students' initiative resulted in the strongest local control over nuclear power plants in the country. Now, the states of California and Montana have adopted similar laws, and in other states and townships, citizens are seeking the same sort of democratic control over the spread of nuclear power.

While the Atomic Energy Act preempts most state laws governing the use of nuclear energy and nuclear waste transport and disposal, several states have had success challenging the scope and focus of the act.

In 1983, the Supreme Court upheld a California moratorium on new nuclear power plants that was based on economic, not safety, concerns. The following year, the Court, in its decision in the Karen Silkwood case, declared that the Atomic Energy Act does not preempt the states' authority to impose punitive damages on nuclear operators.

Massachusetts has a law subjecting the development and operation of nuclear waste disposal sites to public referendum. In addition, many cities, townships, and villages have passed ordinances prohibiting the transport or disposal of nuclear material within their jurisdictions.

PIRG lobbyists know they can usually expect opposition from some special interest group when they begin lobbying on an issue. For example, PIRGs that have pushed for reform of sales practices in the hearing aid and funeral industries have seen those groups mount extensive campaigns to stop the reform. But, unchecked, those industries were taking advantage of consumers. PIRG research revealed that people, mostly elderly, who visit hearing aid dealers are not always adequately evaluated and are often sold expensive devices that don't meet their medical needs. PIRGs have also looked at the funeral industry and found that mourners, naturally under emotional stress, are not given a full range of choices for funeral services.

To address the hearing aid sales problems, PIRGs in Minnesota, Vermont, and New York have lobbied successfully for laws that require hearing aids to be prescribed by medical personnel. And in those states and others, funeral homes may no longer refuse to give prices over the phone or to give customers prices for the least expensive along with the most expensive services.

PIRGs also lobbied in the first states to pass generic drug laws, which say a doctor must indicate on a prescription whether it may be filled with a generic drug instead of a brand-name one. These laws, now in effect in almost every state, were estimated to save consumers a quarter of a billion dollars in 1984.

Other issues addressed through PIRG legislative programs range from environmental protection and property tax reform to access to government records and meetings.

## U.S. PIRG

PIRG efforts in state capitols to pass laws governing such things as hazardous waste management, product safety, and corporate accountability provide citizens of the state with important protections. PIRGs have found, however, that working at the state level alone is not enough. Federal laws can preempt rights that citizens have at the state level. Moreover, there are some issues that are more efficiently handled by federal legislation. In addition to working for federal legislation, a PIRG in the U.S.

## Research and Beyond

capitol can get support from its congressional representatives for PIRG-supported measures at the state level. What's more, a PIRG presence in the nation's capitol can help keep representatives aware of the range of issues citizens in the state are concerned about.

To that end, in 1983 PIRGs from a number of states banded together to create the United States Public Interest Research Group in Washington, D.C. U.S. PIRG combines the skills of lobbyists with extensive community outreach programs in its door-to-door canvass and campus bases to present a strong voice in Washington for initiatives shared by PIRGs nationwide. U.S. PIRG serves as a resource center, offering assistance in organizing and fundraising, and as a clearinghouse for information.

In its first year, U.S. PIRG had a hand in securing voters' rights, promoting legislation that strengthens the program to clean up hazardous waste sites, and helping citizens to represent their interests when utility companies propose huge rate increases or changes in service.

Working from a proposal initiated by CALPIRG, U.S. PIRG developed a "Voter Bill of Rights" and urged the Democratic and Republican parties to adopt it as part of their platforms. The bill is designed to enhance citizen participation by opening up access to registration and voting and by reducing the overarching influence that special-interest political-action-committee money plays in our political process.

The Voter Bill of Rights calls for reforms that include registration by mail, registration on election day, more-convenient polling hours, public financing for congressional campaigns, and the curbing of political action committees to reduce their influence on legislation and increase that of individual voters.

U.S. PIRG Director Gene Karpinski says that, with the voting reform and voter registration projects of PIRGs, "We have the opportunity to put voting back in its proper place; as a right to be respected, rather than a privilege to be earned."

In another project designed to strengthen the citizens' role in policymaking, U.S. PIRG kicked off a national utility reform project in the summer of 1983. The aim of the project is to help local activists establish state-level Citizens' Utility Boards (CUBs) to represent telephone, gas, and electric ratepayers in rate-setting hearings before state regulatory commissions. The state CUBs are voluntarily funded through appeals for contributions included in utility bills. Citizens who join CUB elect a board of directors, which hires the legal and research staff necessary to make cases on behalf of consumers against unneeded rate increases or unfair changes in service. When U.S. PIRG launched the utility reform project, CUBs had been established in only two states. The first CUB was started in 1980 in Wisconsin, and the Illinois state legislature approved a CUB there in 1983. The Wisconsin CUB has helped save consumers $283 million in rate increase requests.

Since then, CUB campaigns have been run in California, Florida, Massachusetts, New York, and several other states. In 1984, the New York Public Service Commission—at the request of Governor Mario Cuomo—approved the creation of a CUB after the legislature refused to pass a CUB bill.

Later that year, the Oregon PIRG launched a citizen initiative to bring a CUB proposal directly to Oregon voters. Utility companies had spent an unprecedented amount of money lobbying to defeat a CUB bill in the legislature the year before, and OSPIRG knew it could not match the resources that would be stacked up against it in another legislative battle.

After a seven-month campaign, during which utility companies spent over $1 million attempting to defeat CUB, Oregon citizens voted 53 percent in favor of it, making Oregon the first state to establish a CUB through popular initiative. Notes Tom Novick, OSPIRG's executive director, "We went with our strength; we knew we couldn't outspend the utility companies, but we also knew that they couldn't out-organize us."

In early 1986, CUBs suffered a setback when the Supreme Court decided that requiring the enclosure of certain solicitations in utility billing envelopes violated the utility companies' First Amendment rights. The case, *Pacific Gas & Electric v. California Public Utility Commission*, involved a ratepayers organization called Toward Utility Rate Normalization (TURN), based in San Francisco.

Tom Tobin, CUB coordinator for U.S. PIRG, points out, however, that "there are several distinctions between the TURN model and the actual CUB model" and says it is unclear how the courts will view these distinctions. While some modifications in the CUB structure may be necessary, he says, CUB proponents remain confident that ratepayers will still be able to band together to counter utility industry clout.

In 1986 U.S PIRG also successfully promoted legislation that strengthens the federal Superfund, which provides money for cleaning up hazardous waste in some of the most dangerous sites identified by the Environmental Protection Agency. It is an issue many PIRGs are taking on in their states, whether through advocating a state-level Superfund or strict rules governing hazardous-waste transportation and disposal.

U.S. PIRG, along with environmental and community groups, backed a stronger version of Superfund to address the growing number of waste sites and the increasing cost of cleaning them up. The U.S. PIRG–supported proposal increased the budget of the Superfund from $1.6 billion to $10 billion, giving the EPA the resources to identify at least 1,600 sites for its priority cleanup list by 1988. The EPA's first priority list contained only 418 sites, compared to the thousands of sites that health officials and citizens' groups suspect are posing a danger to residents living near them.

In October 1986, the lobbying by citizens' groups moved Superfund through Congress and persuaded a reluctant President Reagan to sign the proposal into law.

Another current major focus of U.S. PIRG efforts is the quality of drinking water. The group successfully lobbied for renewal of the Safe Drinking Water Act during the 99th Congress. The bill passed both houses in the summer of 1985 and was reported out of conference in May 1986.

With the legislative victory secure, U.S. PIRG has begun telling citizens how to find out if their drinking water is safe. The recently released *Testing for Toxics: A Guide to Investigating Your Drinking Water* details the ways that consumers can have their drinking water tested for contamination, either by their state health departments or by independent laboratories.

Another priority for U.S. PIRG is a campaign to reform the Price-Anderson Act, a little-known law passed in 1957 that severely reduces the liability of nuclear power plant owners and operators in the event of an accident. The group's Nuclear Accountability Campaign, working with other consumer, environmental, and citizen groups, seeks to ensure that three key objectives are met if a serious nuclear accident were to occur: (1) Provide full compensation for damages to the public. (2) Avoid the use of taxpayer funds for compensating accident victims. (3) Ensure that the nuclear industry is held responsible for damages.

As Kathleen Welch, U.S. PIRG lobbyist and coordinator of the campaign, noted in a *New York Times* op-ed article, "As long as the Price-Anderson liability limits are in place, the door will be open for all industries to demand the same special immunity. Letting industry off the hook for jeopardizing public health and safety is perilous and unacceptable public policy."

U.S. PIRG is also working to inform telephone customers about how the breakup of AT&T affects them. U.S. PIRG is publishing guides to long-distance companies, documenting the effects of the AT&T divestiture on residential telephone users, and lobbying for numerous reforms to make the original divestiture work better for consumers. "Our preliminary research indicates that over twenty percent of low-income consumers can't afford even basic telephone service," states Pamela Gilbert, staff attorney with U.S. PIRG. "If current trends continue, basic service may become unaffordable for even more people."

Finally, U.S. PIRG has been a major force in the campaign to eliminate unnecessary delays by banks in crediting depositors' checks. Its national studies—done in conjunction with state PIRGs—have provided the major documentation on the check-hold problem and have helped prompt legislation to require banks to clear checks within specified periods of time. Bills introduced in Congress would require banks to make funds available within three days of deposit, whereas banks can currently withhold some payments for over two weeks.

Banks usually receive the money on deposited checks overnight, according to U.S. PIRG. Yet, they withhold that money from the depositor for extended periods of time, denying the depositor use of the funds at the same time the bank is earning money on them. Moreover, says the group, very few checks ever bounce, and the vast majority of those are honored on second deposit—a common practice. As a result, the banks have no real justification for withholding depositors' money, says U.S. PIRG.

The goals and strategies of the PIRGS reflect a growing sophistication. Whereas the early PIRG projects required more enthusiasm than expertise, state PIRGs and their national association have in recent years been jumping into battles over complex, technical issues—including nuclear power, utility rate reform, and banking—that require a numbing degree of accuracy and detail. That they have been so successful demonstrates a central tenet of the PIRG philosophy: Anyone can be an "expert." You just have to get involved.

# THREE

# PIRGs in Action

Looking at any PIRG project, whether in the legislature, the courts, or the community, one can see that no effort is isolated. Lobbying requires research and writing as well as organizing in the community. Studies issued by PIRGs do not just outline the problem, they propose solutions that range from legislation to community education. Community organizing focuses on legislative proposals or the study findings. So, while the projects can be categorized as to their major component, students have learned it is the well-rounded efforts that use the variety of the PIRG resources that will succeed.

Here are some case histories that bear that out.

## STUDENTS BATTLE FOR A BOTTLE BILL

In 1973, a student from Hampshire College in western Massachusetts went on a long bicycle trip through Oregon. Throughout, he was struck by the distinct absence of broken bottles and cans along the roadside, a most welcome change of scenery from the Bay State. What accounted for the difference in the way people in the two states were disposing of their used containers?

The student discovered the answer was the so-called

bottle bill. In 1971 Oregon had become the first state to pass a bill requiring consumers to pay a deposit on beer and soda cans, plastic containers, and bottles. With the bottle bill in effect, people could turn their empties into money. In addition, the used containers would become available for recycling. Hence, the law served two purposes: It kept the state cleaner and contributed to conservation of resources.

The student returned to school and persuaded his campus PIRG chapter and the statewide PIRG Board of Directors to endorse the enactment of a Massachusetts bottle bill. Thus began one of the fiercest battles on public interest legislation in Massachusetts history, one that involved thousands of students and citizens in a campaign that lasted nine years.

Getting a bottle bill on the books is never a small task. Traditionally, bottle bills have come under attack from a powerful alliance: bottle and can manufacturers, soda bottlers, beer brewers, distributors, retailers, and labor unions. They are willing and able to finance high-priced campaigns against the bills.

Mindy Lubber, who helped coordinate the campaign from 1976 through its victory in 1982, joined MASSPIRG in August of '76. Before coming to Massachusetts, Lubber had been on NYPIRG's Board of Directors while earning a Bachelor of Arts and Masters in Business Administration at the State University of New York at Buffalo. When she arrived at MASSPIRG, she had just three months before the bottle bill was to be voted on in a November ballot. After failing to get the bill passed by the legislature in 1974, MASSPIRG had formed a coalition with other state groups, and by 1975, gathered the one hundred thousand signatures needed to put the issue on a ballot. In those months before the November vote, Lubber directed students, who informed the public about the issue by canvassing door to door and telephoning, and promoted press coverage.

MASSPIRG spent about $40,000 on the '76 ballot campaign. The coalition of groups that opposed the bill—such as the Massachusetts Soft Drink Association (which represents soft drink wholesalers and retailers), beer manufacturers across the nation, retail store owners, and container manufacturers—spent more than $2 million. Despite being so greatly outspent, backers of the initiative lost by only 8/10 of 1 percent. MASSPIRG believed the public interest had not been served. The merits of bottle bill legislation had been proven in other states where the law was in effect, but just enough voters had been deceived by the beverage industry's claims to the contrary. So MASSPIRG went back to the legislature.

The electoral campaign in 1976 had made the bottle bill a statewide concern. For the next two years, MASSPIRG capitalized on the issue's visibility and gathered support from public officials and the media. The group found endorsements for the bottle bill from then Governor Michael Dukakis and his secretaries of Economic, Environmental, and Consumer Affairs, and from ten newspapers in the state, which ran editorials in favor of the bill.

Students worked each semester during those years talking before community groups and generating letters and phone calls to legislators and editors of local newspapers. This outreach informed the community about the bottle bill, and let legislators know where their constituents stood. John McGlynn, who began working for MASSPIRG on the bottle bill issue as a student at Boston College and later became the campus organizer at Southeastern Massachusetts University, said "students were the backbone of the campaign." In southeast Massachusetts, residents were skeptical and less supportive of the bottle bill than residents anywhere else in the state. McGlynn said most people there believed industry's contention that jobs would be lost if the legislation passed. Students held community meetings and spoke on radio programs to let residents know how successful the law had been in other states. As a result, support for the bottle bill in that area eventually grew by 20 percent from the 1976 ballot to 1982, when the issue was to be put before the voters once more.

In 1979, the bottle bill was finally passed by the legislature and sent to the governor's office. However, the newly elected governor, Edward King, vetoed the bill, despite a recommendation from his own task force that it be approved. That legislative session ended without further action on the bill.

It was reintroduced in 1981, temporarily "bottled up" in the Senate because of stepped-up pressure by anti-bottle bill forces, then finally passed to the governor. King once again vetoed it. With an override of a governor's veto requiring two-thirds support in both the House and the Senate, "Anybody who had any political wisdom wouldn't have thought we could turn this thing around," Lubber says. Not only was the governor against the bill, but the very powerful speaker of the House and the president of the Senate also opposed it. MASSPIRG knew it was up against incredible odds, but as Lubber points out, "The veto was wrong; clearly, the people wanted a bottle bill." Polls showed 70 percent of Massachusetts residents supported the bottle bill. That kept MASSPIRG at work despite the odds.

During the two weeks following the veto, students and volunteers for other groups working with MASSPIRG met with editorial boards and continued to receive endorsements for the bill from major newspapers. MASSPIRG lobbyists kept at work in the capitol. But the most important part of the veto override campaign was MASSPIRG's personal contact, as volunteers went door to door to speak with people at their homes. This allowed MASSPIRG to counter industry claims about job loss resulting from the bill, and to publicize a study by Governor King's own Office of Economic Affairs, which indicated twenty-two hundred jobs would be created.

MASSPIRG was also able to point to polls in states such as Vermont, Maine, and Connecticut that showed 80 to 90 percent of the people liked container deposit laws after they were passed. That discounted another suggestion by industry that, once in effect, the law would prove ineffective and unpopular. During those two weeks, MASSPIRG spurred fifteen thousand contacts to the legislature.

The legislators responded. Twenty-seven representatives and nine senators switched their votes to support the bill, enough for the two-thirds margin needed to override the governor's veto. However, the beverage industry wouldn't take yes for an answer. It mounted a campaign to have the bill repealed through a referendum. Getting a proposal to repeal legislation on the ballot requires fewer signatures than does putting an issue to an initial vote. That worked in the opponents' favor. And, since many retailers opposed it, they posted petitions in their stores and got the necessary signatures without much footwork. But the footwork that had worked for MASSPIRG before worked again. Relying on volunteers "armed with the facts," MASSPIRG went back to the community and successfully urged people to defend the measure on the November 1982 ballot. With 59 percent of the votes cast against repeal of the bottle bill, the issue drew more votes than four other referenda on that ballot, including one dealing with the death penalty and a nuclear freeze resolution. In January 1983, the bottle bill went into effect in Massachusetts.

As in any long campaign, the amount of time students spent on the bottle bill fluctuated from year to year. Lubber, a full-time staff person, had to divide her time between the bottle bill and several other MASSPIRG projects. However, with Lubber keeping abreast of the issue, MASSPIRG was able to mobilize plenty of students when the issue came to the forefront and volunteers were needed in the communities and the capitol. Even though it sometimes looked as though MASSPIRG did not have a chance against the political machinations in the state capitol, "We never considered backing off," Lubber says. "The bill is such a logical measure . . . the public wanted it."

The majority did anyway. Milt Segal was in the minority, though. Segal is former president of the Massachusetts Food Association, which represents retail and wholesale food suppliers. He worked against the bottle bill "for ten years, until Mindy Lubber and her crowd" prevailed, he says good-naturedly.

When MASSPIRG first began promoting the bill, Segal said he didn't think too much of a group of students getting involved. Now, thirteen years later, he realizes he did not take them seriously enough. While he is quick to point out that he still does not agree with the container deposit law, he is just as quick to note his respect for Lubber and the work done by MASSPIRG.

"Did MASSPIRG do a good job? Yes," Segal says. "I didn't agree with everything they said during the campaign but that's part of the battle. I've seen the quality of the work they do improve in the last few years." Segal adds that on future issues, "I'd want to have them on my side."

Lubber says that the bottle bill effort has given MASSPIRG a new respectability not only in the eyes of industry, but in the legislature and community as well. The legislators know that MASSPIRG will be in touch with their constituents, and the community knows the group is working to make sure the public's interests are truly represented.

In addition, the bill provided hundreds of students

over the years with skills in research, writing, fundraising, meeting with the press, public debate, and polling. Lubber said students also saw first hand that citizens can take on a multimillion-dollar industry and win.

MASSPIRG Director Doug Phelps says, in a considerable understatement, that the group's work on the bottle bill "shows we're resilient, that we don't take on an issue and drop it."

Steve Urban, editorial page editor of *The Standard-Times*, in southeast Massachusetts, said, judging from letters to the editor he has received, people in his part of the state—the area where residents were previously least supportive—like the bottle bill. Urban, who wrote the paper's editorial in favor of the bill, says the law is "like being told to eat your vegetables; you may not want to, but once you do, it isn't so bad." He noted that one supermarket chain that had been opposed to the bottle bill took out ads in *The Standard-Times* after the bill had become law, saying it would do all it could to make the law work. In addition, his paper reported, five months after the law went into effect, that the State Public Works Department announced litter along Massachusetts highways was down by 30 percent—except in towns bordering states with no deposit law.

Just three months after the law went into effect, the Boston Marathon provided an unexpected measuring stick of the law's effectiveness. In the past, when the several thousand runners and the crowds were gone, cans and bottles were strewn about and served as a reminder of the marathon's path. However, that year, Lubber said, MASSPIRG received calls from people accustomed to seeing the post-race litter who said "the bottle bill works!" They reported seeing youngsters collecting the now recyclable bottles and cans, leaving the area unusually free of litter.

## HELPING MILLWORKERS BREATHE EASIER

> Those who hackle in the flax and hemp to prepare it for being spun and wove, afford frequent instance of unwholesomeness of their trade; for there flies out of this matter a foul and mischievous powder, that entering the lungs by mouth and throat, causes continual coughs and gradually makes way for asthma. . . . But at the long run if they find their affliction grows upon them they must look out for another trade; for 'tis a sordid profit that's accompanied with the destruction of health.

That description of a disease known as byssinosis, which also strikes workers exposed to cotton dust, was written in 1705. In 1973, more than two and one-half centuries later, members of the North Carolina Public Interest Research Group found that as far as most textile workers and much of the medical community in the United States were concerned, the disease had never been discovered. Not that workers in the textile industry were immune to byssinosis, or "brown lung"; they were just uninformed about its symptoms. Doctors tended to overlook it as a possible diagnosis, ignoring the specific disease that cotton dust can cause. In fact, in the early seventies newspapers were still referring to it as a "disease *alleged* to exist." That was the attitude of many legislators and public health officials as well. And industry's attitude was reflected in a mid-1960s statement by a textile manufacturers' association. It acknowledged the disease existed, but said that people of the Third World and other "weaker" peoples were subject to it—not American workers. The Occupational Safety and Health Administration adopted industry's standards for the amount of dust allowable in the air of the mills, shortly after the agency was established by Congress in 1970. OSHA termed development of its own standards a top priority, yet industry's standards, which NCPIRG and the Textile Workers Union believed were inadequate, remained in place until 1980.

With one-third of the nation's 950,000 textile workers living in North Carolina, making OSHA more accountable for millworkers' health was an ideal project for NCPIRG.

Thad Moore, a student who had organized a PIRG at Wake Forest College, authored NCPIRG's first report on brown lung, in 1974. The report dealt with the basic question of whether conditions in a textile mill can cause the disease. When asked why he got involved in the issue of brown lung, he says, "I'm a native of North Carolina." On its face, the answer may seem disingenuous—but to Moore, living in North Carolina meant living around mills and mill workers all his life, and he is naturally concerned about workers' health.

By the early 1970s, evidence was mounting that byssinosis was a distinct disease caused by inhaling cotton particles. But, Moore says, "At the time, you couldn't talk to any medical doctor or anyone who even knew anything about it," despite American and British studies on the issue. In America, studies of millworkers found that the incidence of brown lung is from 12 to 29 percent of all workers, with rates of up to 41 percent in the more dusty areas of the mill. In England, studies were so conclusive that worker compensation laws have covered compensation for brown lung disease since the 1930s. The human costs of the disease are severe. Years of inhaling the dust results in labored breathing, coughing, and ultimately chronic pulmonary lung disease, similar to chronic bronchitis or emphysema.

While Moore was compiling his report, NCPIRG sought to add a dozen amendments to a proposal to create a state-run OSHA that was being considered by the legislature. The state legislature did accept two of them—dealing with worker access to health records and protection for workers who file complaints about safety violations in the workplace. But for the most part, the state-level OSHA, created quickly and without much fanfare, was not designed to be any tougher on the problem of byssinosis than the federal agency.

In the fall of 1973, NCPIRG adopted a three-step strategy: community education, worker health screenings, and lobbying for more stringent rules to protect workers.

While NCPIRG brought the problem of cotton dust to the attention of workers and the general community, "It became clear that we needed a separate organization to be a full-time advocate on this issue, whose membership could include textile workers and the community," Wib Gulley, then-NCPIRG director, says. Because of that need, Thad Moore and Mike Spock, working with NCPIRG, conceived of the Brown Lung Association in 1974. The BLA quickly expanded to South Carolina, Georgia, and Alabama, and worked with the PIRG, the union, and the community. Dr. James A. Merchant, then a fellow studying business at Duke University's School of Public Health, notes that the groups, by working together, made the Department of Labor and the Industrial Commission "aware that byssinosis was an issue workers were concerned with," and that the groups would "hold officials accountable for worker protection."

First, the PIRG, working with the Brown Lung Association, organized a large conference on brown lung in 1974. The conference brought together experts from around the country to introduce North Carolina doctors, nurses, public health officials, and people from the textile industry to the cause, diagnosis, treatment, and prevention of the disease. Most health care professionals were never taught about byssinosis, so they would diagnose its symptoms as other respiratory ailments. Many claimed the symptoms were the result of cigarette smoking by patients. Even if a doctor believed cotton dust was hurting a worker's health, the worker had no recourse but to quit his job, and perhaps receive small disability payments from Social Security. The situation Lacy L. Wright found himself in illustrates the dilemma workers faced.

In 1962, after forty years in the mill, Wright began having problems breathing. By 1966, his doctor told Wright he had emphysema and that he had to quit smoking and working in cotton dust. Wright worked in an area of the mill where the bales of cotton are broken open and prepared for spinning into thread. "I saw times [in the mill] where it looked like there was a heavy fog," he says. In the steamy heat, masks the workers were supposed to wear got so clogged with dust that they could not be worn. Though Wright did not understand the toxic effects of byssinosis, he notes that he "talked to plant managers about cotton dust as far back as nineteen and fifty-five . . . that it was hurting people. Naturally, they brushed it aside. They didn't want to pay out any money." His only choice when he found out the cotton dust had indeed disabled him was to quit the mill, at age sixty-two. "As far as your breathing is concerned, it's hard to tell whether you've got brown lung or something else," Wright explains. "The workings of brown lung and the workings of emphysema are similar." Yet Wright learned making the distinction would be important. Since the emphysema was caused in part by the mill work, Social Security would have paid him disability benefits, but Wright's other activity— his farm work—would have been restricted. "I had twelve hundred or so chickens, and I couldn't afford to hire nobody to look after them, and [disability payment restrictions] wouldn't let me look after them myself and still get disability." So Wright, with no worker compensation to turn to, began drawing small retirement payments from Social Security and tending his chickens.

Once the North Carolina legislature finally revised the compensation laws to specifically include victims of byssinosis, NCPIRG wanted to identify doctors and nurses who were concerned about the disease and who could diagnose workers accurately. "It was a major hurdle just to get doctors to say, 'Yes, you may have it,'" Moore says. NCPIRG set up free medical screening services for textile workers, with the help of the Brown Lung Association. The screening services alerted workers if they were afflicted with the disease and distributed information about how to recognize brown lung and how to apply for compensation.

Wright, who had become president of the first BLA chapter in Greensboro, discovered through one of those screenings that he had byssinosis himself. He was later awarded worker compensation.

"There's an old saying," Wright says, "that 'you don't need somebody to tell you you can't get your breath.'" What workers did need was someone to tell them the reason they could not get their breath, and that the company was responsible. "If a person had a breathing problem, and had worked in the dust, we helped get them signed up for compensation," Wright explains.

Few claims for brown lung had been filed in the state before NCPIRG began the screenings, but as workers began to realize that their shortness of breath or chest pains could be the result of the dusty air they breathed day after day, a virtual torrent of claims was filed—hundreds after the first month of NCPIRG's education project. According to Dr. Merchant, NCPIRG "played an important role in . . . educating workers and involving the lay press" in the issue. Prior to NCPIRG's involvement, the topic of byssinosis had been "pretty much a research question," Merchant says.

By 1975, NCPIRG began working with the Institute for Southern Studies to launch the third part of its brown lung project—a five-month study of the North Carolina Department of Labor and its implementation of OSHA standards. Two staff members and several student interns scrutinized more than one hundred inspection reports and case files at the Department of Labor. The findings were published in a report titled *Caution: NCOSHA Is Dangerous to Your Health*. As the title suggests, the report found widespread negligence within the state agency. NCOSHA claimed that the state's working conditions were generally safe, yet its own files documented that 86 percent of the textile companies inspected by NCOSHA personnel in 1974 were in violation of federal standards. The report revealed that fines were not often levied on offenders, and when they were, they tended to be low—about one-third the amount levied on cotton dust offenders in other states. The report also documented the NCOSHA director's willingness to excuse and cooperate with industry offenders. The state OSHA blamed budget constraints for any inspection shortcomings. But NCPIRG understood that even if state budget problems were resolved, federal cotton dust standards were still not strong enough to protect workers.

So, NCPIRG continued its project, joining with the Textile Workers Union of America to file a formal petition with the federal OSHA requesting that the agency finally set a more stringent standard than the lenient industry standard it had been using since its inception. Although setting a standard had allegedly been a priority at OSHA when it was formed, the agency was now using it as a political football. It was revealed in Senate Watergate hearings that then-OSHA Director George Guenther, not willing to offend powerful political allies in industry, wrote in a 1972 memo that "no highly controversial standards—i.e. cotton dust, etc.—will be proposed by OSHA or NIOSH [National Institute of Safety and Health, the research arm of OSHA]" as part of a program "to promote the advantages of four more years of properly managed OSHA for use in the [Nixon re-election] campaign." NIOSH did propose a nonbinding cotton dust criteria, but NCPIRG and the Textile Workers Union filed a lawsuit to compel the secretary of labor "to initiate and conclude formal proceedings" to establish more stringent regulation of cotton particles.

With all of NCPIRG's efforts to get workers who were afflicted with brown lung to file compensation claims, textile industry officials were beginning to see it would be costly *not* to clean up the air in the mills. And, according to John Lumsden, former head of the Occupational Health Branch of the North Carolina Department of Health, NCPIRG's campaign informed the broader population about brown lung as well. "NCPIRG certainly did raise awareness. They had access to the news media that state offices and the textile industry did not have," Lumsden says.

In 1978, President Carter's OSHA proposed a cotton dust standard similar to the one that PIRG and the union were proposing. Yet making the standard an official regulation is a lengthy process, and before some aspects were finalized, the antiregulation Reagan administration came into office. Reagan's OSHA is seeking to exempt some industries, such as knitting, from the standard altogether because it concludes there have been no signs of damage to worker health in those areas, and to reduce medical surveillance in some cases. OSHA is also trying to push back the deadline for compliance in some areas of industry by two years. The Reagan administration also proposed revisions to the cotton dust rule in 1981 that would require "cost-benefit" analyses to be conducted on the regulations. The U.S. Supreme Court, however, struck down the revisions and ordered OSHA to promulgate the rules without a cost-benefit analysis requirement. After proposing additional revisions in June 1983 (which resulted in some minor compromises on the rule), the final rule was issued on December 10, 1985.

Dr. Merchant, now a professor of epidemiology and public medicine at the University of Iowa College of Medicine, says there is ample evidence that worker health is endangered in textile-related industries, and he states that OSHA should maintain vigorous medical screenings. He also believes industry, already in 80-percent compliance with the Carter administration standard, does have the technology to meet standards in all areas of the mill. Obviously there is more to be done to ensure that OSHA implements adequate standards: That is why it is important to have the BLA established and continuing to educate workers and keep the issue before the public. So, while NCPIRG moves on to other issues, its impact will be felt for years to come in North Carolina communities and in the healthier atmosphere of the mills.

## CALPIRG AND THE MEAT SCANDAL

A sense of drama exists in many PIRG projects. Students and staff know that their efforts can lead to major changes in public policies, and can help thousands of people. That kind of excitement is part of the reason students get involved. But in one case, a PIRG project had more than its share of drama, including most of the elements of a good Hollywood movie—discreet rendezvous with informants, office break-ins, threats, late-night phone calls—even FBI investigations resulting in convictions. Where else but in California?

The project started routinely. California PIRG in San Diego had always been active in food policy, doing cost and quality comparisons between stores in the San Diego area. The community looked to CALPIRG for reliable studies; even the markets took notice. One supermarket chain, found by CALPIRG to have the highest prices in the area, cut its prices substantially, then launched an advertising campaign with headlines such as "We hear you, CALPIRG."

CALPIRG's involvement with problems in meat pricing and quality began in 1973. In that year and in 1974, CALPIRG investigated the fat content in ground beef at area supermarkets, and partially as a result of those studies, the state attorney general's office filed litigation against a major retailer.

So it was not unusual for consumers to turn to CALPIRG with complaints about meat. What was unusual was the course that followed when a CALPIRG volunteer brought Frank Hogya's allegation to the group in 1975.

George Schultz, then a third-year law student at the University of San Diego, had become involved in CALPIRG in a small way. He spent some of his free time helping CALPIRG recycle cans and put up signs on campus promoting the group and its activities. Schultz, who was also a clerk at a law office, did not have time to do much more with CALPIRG. All that changed when retired Navy Chief Frank Hogya walked into the law office of William Bauer, where Schultz was clerking, and started talking about meat.

Hogya had been following the meat industry for years in southern California. A man in search of a good steak, he knew meat grading procedures and he knew that cattle were being cross-bred to create hardier stock. As a result, they were yielding lower-quality steaks. Yet the commissary where Hogya shopped continued to carry as much meat labeled "choice" as ever. He had studied USDA manuals and grades of meat and could tell by looking at the product in the store that it did not meet the standards its government-approved stamp indicated it should. Hogya was also, as Schultz was to write later, in search of justice:

> "When I enlisted in the Navy, I took an oath to protect the nation from its enemies, both foreign and domestic," [Hogya] says in a firm, deep voice. "We took care of the foreign ones. Now we've got to get some of the domestic ones."

## PIRGs in Action

Hogya had been trying to stir action on the problem for several years, calling and writing federal officials and legislators. Bauer had served as Hogya's attorney in a previous, unrelated case, so Hogya went back to him for help. Bauer decided to have his law clerk, Schultz, spend some time looking into Hogya's allegations.

Schultz remembers thinking that Hogya was too preoccupied with the details of the beef industry. But Schultz began knocking on doors, talking to meat graders, and getting the names of other people who could give information, including a meat grader convicted of taking bribes to give low-quality meat an undeserved higher grade. From there, the investigation snowballed, or meatballed, as the case may be, and Schultz realized Hogya was right on target.

Since Schultz was familiar with CALPIRG's work, he took his findings to the group. He knew that if CALPIRG was involved it would lend the investigation credibility. "If Frank Hogya says things are messed up in the beef industry, people will say 'Who is Frank Hogya?' But if CALPIRG says things are messed up, people will listen," Schultz said. CALPIRG staff remembered the many complaints they had received on the meat industry, and they were ready to get involved in this case.

The union proved to be a wise one. The press coverage CALPIRG received on its study of the hamburger labeling brought sources out of the woodwork to expose other unfair and illegal practices. Often these "meat throats," as the informants came to be called, were afraid for their jobs and even their safety. Their meetings with Schultz were elaborately planned to avoid being discovered. Schultz recalls once meeting an employee of a meatpacking house alongside the interstate while the informant pretended to have car trouble. For another meeting, Schultz was instructed to go two hundred miles out into the California desert area where he sat under a cactus at high noon while the informant named the names of people who were giving bribes and those who were accepting them.

"It was scary sometimes," Schultz says. He knew he was one of a few people walking around with information that could indict many people in the beef industry. He received threats, and Bauer's law office was broken into and the beef files were ransacked. But it was knowing that the industry was "running scared" that confirmed for CALPIRG the fact that it was on to something big.

CALPIRG's investigations, and subsequent monitoring by the Justice Department, brought these situations to light:

- The major meatpackers in the state had been meeting every Wednesday and arbitrarily setting the wholesale price of meat. In late 1976 and early 1977 Schultz began gathering bits of information from his sources about "the Wednesday meetings," and "something strange going on" with the announcements of meat prices, and finally one source's guess that prices were being illegally set each week. Schultz reported the information to the FBI.
- The California attorney general's office subpoenaed records of telephone calls, invoices, and other information from nineteen southern California meat packers in its investigation of price fixing and upgrading.
- The secretary of agriculture announced a major investigation of all aspects of meat pricing in both the wholesale and retail market.
- Schultz was invited to meet with the assistant secretary of consumer affairs for USDA and Senator Lawton Chiles to discuss the problem. He also testified for CALPIRG before the U.S. Con-

gress Committee on Small Business Affairs and other committees.
- CBS's *60 Minutes* did a segment on the meat scandal called "Bum Steer." They took a respected USDA official to a local supermarket to determine if the quality of meat offered for sale matched its label. A FedMart official responsible for that company's meat buying was asked to resign after misgraded beef was discovered in the *60 Minutes* search. Dan Rather, then with *60 Minutes*, said of the investigation: "Government officials called [the piece] lots of things: Some stung by charges of government inefficiency called it unfortunate reporting while others applauded it and used it to initiate administrative changes to help protect consumers and encourage fairer competition."
- Eventually thirteen were convicted on charges of price fixing or of falsely labeling lower quality meat as higher grade.

With the volume of evidence in, CALPIRG, with Schultz and Bauer now serving as its attorneys, filed a class action suit against the meat packers on behalf of southern California consumers who had been paying inflated prices, as much as 20 percent more per pound, because of the price fixing and mislabeling. The suit asked for $6 billion in damages from the packers and supermarkets at fault. To bolster the attorneys' efforts, students did surveys of supermarkets to see what grades of meat they carried, and they surveyed wholesale meat distributors.

Shortly after the suit was filed, a U.S. Supreme Court ruling changed the climate for the California suit. In the Supreme Court case, the state of Illinois discovered that price fixing in the brick industry had boosted the cost of several buildings by millions of dollars. When the state sued the brick company, the Court ruled that only the party directly affected by the cost increase could sue. In this case, that would have been the general contractor for the buildings, yet it had no cause to sue because its bill to the state covered the cost of the bricks, no matter how inflated that cost was. In California, it meant that only supermarkets or other meat retailers could sue for the price fixing. However, they were not damaged either since they just passed on the inflated prices to consumers.

With that Supreme Court decision, it seemed as if CALPIRG's case for the consumers did not have a chance. Schultz and Bauer realized they would need a change of the law in the state before consumers could have any recourse against unfair wholesaler prices, and before the suit against the meat packers could have a chance. With CALPIRG there to lobby the state legislature, such a solution was not out of the question.

So CALPIRG quietly promoted legislation to change the law in the state, while the lawsuit was put on a back burner. The Supreme Court rule applied to federal antitrust law, CALPIRG reasoned, and that left room for the state to make its own version. Schultz said the CALPIRG effort was deliberately low-key because if the group had promoted the bill as "consumer legislation," high-powered industry lobbying groups would have moved to delay or squelch it. CALPIRG pointed out to legislators that the law was necessary to protect taxpayers from being "ripped off" as they were in Illinois.

The bill passed unanimously. But by now the Court would not allow CALPIRG to file its suit, with the judge saying the delay, caused by CALPIRG's waiting to see if the law would be passed, was damaging to the defendants. Yet CALPIRG has seen the law benefit other groups: Schultz reports that he has received calls from lawyers all over the state who said the law would allow them to bring suits for consumers they could not have brought before, such as one against wheelchair manufacturers who were allegedly fixing prices. As for meat in San Diego stores, Schultz says supermarket chains are no longer carrying meat with labels that command a higher price by misrepresenting quality.

While the meat investigation was not the typical PIRG project that relied directly on the work of many students, Schultz says the case was given credibility from the beginning because it was associated with CALPIRG. Because of the quality work done by students in the past on food surveys, that association was a positive one. Also, CALPIRG was able to generate publicity for the case, it had useful contacts in government agencies and consumer groups, and the law it lobbied for, as a result of the meat case, helped consumers statewide. "That one bill is going to have more effect in the long run than winning the suit against the meat industry would have," Schultz said.

Schultz went on to crusade against meat industry pricing abuses and to co-author, with Wayne Swanson, a book in 1982 about the scandal in California and meat industry problems nationwide. They called it *Prime Rip*. Schultz became a partner in Bauer's law firm, and he still appears on TV and radio talk shows to discuss the scandal. While the investigation's drama has not generated the interest of any big-time movie producers, Dan Rather wrote in the book's forward: "If Mr. Schultz ever decides to leave the law, I will try to have him hired by CBS News."

## TRUTH IN TESTING

For years now, students have weaved their way through a maze of standardized tests. A virtual alphabet soup of tests punctuates one's education—PSAT/NMSQT, SAT, LSAT, MCAT, and GRE. As students pursue higher degrees, the scene becomes familiar: A roomful of people are told to enter their names and their identification numbers on computer forms; they are told how much time they should spend on each section of the test, they are told they will be permitted to go to the restroom only one at a time. What they are not told is that their performance on a single test could shape their future.

The majority of the tests are designed and administered by a single corporation, the Educational Testing Service (ETS). The corporation's power is far-reaching, as shown in this excerpt from a Ralph Nader report titled "The Reign of ETS—The Corporation that Makes Up Minds":

> Thirty years after its founding ETS could claim to influence, among other things, the chance to go to half of American colleges, 75 percent of the graduate programs and 100 percent of the law schools; the opportunity to sell insurance in Illinois, fight fire or walk a police beat in Philadelphia, become an officer in the Liberian Merchant Marine, practice law in forty-two states, or receive a scholarship from the State of Georgia, Union Carbide, or the Brotherhood of Steamfitters. Every year, seven to nine million people trying to advance through thousands of educational institutions and fifty different occupations are judged by a multiple-choice test, written according to the directions of one looseleaf manual stored at ETS.

Few people know how much rests on an ETS test score. Until recently, students did not even know much about the test itself—what it measured, how accurately it predicted future success, what was told to the schools about the meaning of the test results. Students never knew which questions they answered correctly, and which ones they got wrong. The New York Public Interest Research Group made a simple request of ETS: Provide test-takers with more information about their scores and their significance. ETS was not anxious to comply. But after four years and a massive NYPIRG campaign, a truth-in-testing law passed in New York State. The truth-in-testing measure requires the testing industry to: make public internal studies on the test's validity and data relating to possible cultural and class biases contained in the test; give students specific information on what their scores mean and how their scores are presented to educational and other institutions; provide students, on request, with a copy of the questions, correct answers, and students' own answers thirty days after receipt of the request.

NYPIRG first looked into ETS in 1975 when the corporation lost the test scores of at least two hundred students who took the law school entrance examination. NYPIRG set up complaint centers on New York campuses to collect information from students about specific problems they had with the testing service. Further studies by NYPIRG and Nader researcher Allan Nairn found that students from low-income families routinely scored lower than those from high-income families; the lower the income, the lower the average score. Standardized testing biases related to these results were reported as early as 1952 in a report by the Commission on Financing Higher Education, which stated that "these tests systematically penalize working class youth, because the test problems are more familiar to middle-class than to working-class experience. . . ." Clearly, low-income students were at a disadvantage going into the tests. In addition, studies of the grade point averages and economic background of college freshmen concluded, "The income of the student's parents has no relationship to freshman GPA . . ."

As these facts came to light, it was clear that reform was in order. And, as Ralph Nader later wrote in a September 21, 1979, column, the testing industry should be held accountable for more than lost test scores: "Certainly it would help students to realize that these tests do *not* measure determination, judgment, idealism, or creativity—the human attributes responsible for human progress."

Once NYPIRG went to the community to explain the issue, it gained tremendous support. Students spoke to parents' organizations, minority groups, and teachers, and they met with reporters and the editorial boards of local newspapers and submitted articles to campus papers. Student clubs and ethnic associations offered resolutions calling for passage of the truth-in-testing law. In the meantime, NYPIRG Director Donald Ross found a sponsor for the bill: Republican Senator Kenneth LaValle, from eastern Long Island. LaValle had been a teacher and high school principal, and the position he would later occupy in the Senate proved invaluable in passing the bill. Mary-Ann McLean-Austen, counsel to the senator, recalls that when he decided to sponsor the bill, she was a "reluctant soldier" at first. But she became a strong proponent of testing reform when she "started reading NYPIRG's very convincing arguments" countering those of ETS.

All of this support finally led to the first legislative hearings on the proposal in the spring of 1978. Ed Hanley, a legislative intern, was there and testified. However, the legislature took no further action that session. In preparation for the 1979 session, Allan Nairn helped NYPIRG document the problems with ETS, and joined NYPIRG in lobbying for the bill. ETS began to feel pressure from NYPIRG's efforts, and prepared for the upcoming legislative battle by hiring two high-priced law firms to bolster its lobbying efforts.

During the floor debate in the Assembly, Representative John J. Flanagan, Republican of Huntington, made an impassioned plea for the bill's passage: "Standardized tests are taking over our evaluation of people," he charged. "Maybe we can't get rid of that but . . . we have to . . . open up the process." The bill passed the Assembly, but still faced an uphill battle in the Senate.

The truth-in-testing bill was debated before the Senate

Higher Education Committee, which the bill's sponsor, Kenneth LaValle, chaired. Nairn recalls that the PIRG "shocked ETS and many of the politicians because NYPIRG lined up twenty-five to thirty witnesses" to testify. Witnesses included Lewis Pike, a former ETS test developer now with the National Institute of Education; Walter Haney, staff director of a national testing group; representatives from the NAACP and other groups; and students and parents. In the hearing, NYPIRG testimony was able to disprove many of ETS's claims about the effects of the bill.

Throughout the legislative session, NYPIRG's work continued at three levels. Nairn and Steve Cary, a NYPIRG legislative intern, worked in Albany to promote the bill. NYPIRG students went back to the individuals and groups they had seen earlier, urging them to write and call their representatives. Other students held press conferences to counter ETS's claims. In general the press coverage was good, which Nairn attributed to NYPIRG's efforts to meet with editorial boards to convince them the testing bill was important to their readers.

The lobbying effort was intense. The bill was voted out of the Senate Higher Education Committee and sent to the Republican-controlled conference committee, which would determine whether it would go to the floor for a vote. The Senate majority leader, Warren Anderson, would often kill bills by keeping them from the floor. Nairn knew getting Anderson's support, or at least keeping him from actively opposing the bill, was crucial. ETS knew that too, and sent a Cornell professor to persuade Anderson that the truth-in-testing law would hinder universities in selecting students qualified for college. Nairn and NYPIRG countered with their findings that high school grades were actually a better predictor of how well one would do at college than were the standardized tests. NYPIRG was able to rebut all of the arguments made by ETS, and Anderson let the bill go to the floor for a vote.

"ETS was really alarmed," Nairn says. It began sending memos to legislators predicting, among other things, that the reform measure would cause the corporation to stop administering tests in New York, saying the costs of the tests would become prohibitive. Nairn and NYPIRG issued a rebuttal of ETS's claim, using the corporation's own internal documents to prove their case. The lobbying went on at a fever pitch. ETS tried to portray NYPIRG as uninformed about the intricacies of "psychometric" testing. But, as Hanley says, "We had our experts and could answer any ETS charges."

ETS poured on the pressure in other ways. One "political heavyweight," a lobbyist for an association representing private colleges, sent LaValle a memo of opposition to truth-in-testing, parroting the ETS reasons for opposing the bill. NYPIRG met with the lobbyist to go over the memo point by point and he went from fiery opposition to lukewarm endorsement of the bill.

Next, using its ample resources, ETS unleashed an intensive mailing campaign, sending out thousands of form letters for people to sign and send to their legislators. NYPIRG's constituent work stepped up then, contacting PTA chapters, student organizations, prominent educators, and individual parents and teachers to generate letters in support of the truth-in-testing legislation.

Although the truth-in-testing law would cost the state a negligible amount, the bill got sent to the Senate Ways and Means Committee as a stalling tactic. The committee planned to issue a report echoing ETS's line—without really evaluating the financial impact the bill would have. NYPIRG learned of this and complained to the legislators on the committee. When the staff report was released, it simply stated that the bill had no financial implication for the state.

*PIRGs in Action*

Nairn remembers that at the last minute, when the Ways and Means Committee was preparing to vote, an ETS lawyer "raced around the committee room giving senators copies of what they said was a compromise allegedly worked out with the opposition." Nairn promptly followed the attorney around the room, saying, "No, this is not a compromise we've agreed to." Instead of proceeding with the vote, the senators then decided to have a debate. Following that, the committee finally sent the bill to the Senate floor.

As the final days of the session drew near, "I must have heard 'the bill is dead' a dozen times during those last two weeks," Nairn says. It came down to the last day of the session and the bill still hadn't been called for a vote. It was not until evening that a vote was called; ETS lobbyists began persuading members to avoid voting by going to dinner. Then the Democratic leadership used delaying tactics while runners went to restaurants, calling the dining members back for the vote. The bill passed, and at 11:30 p.m., it was sent to the governor.

With the legislative battle over, NYPIRG turned its attention to the governor's office. Governor Hugh Carey had indicated that he was "inclined" to support the bill, but still had reservations and remained undecided.

Thousands of letters poured into Carey's office. The issue was covered on the front page of *The New York Times* and on national news broadcasts. The fate of the bill was indefinite right up to the governor's deadline for signing it. He was on vacation by that time, but he had the bill flown to him, and his signature made truth-in-testing the law. At the signing, Carey said, "The bill's requirements open to public scrutiny, review, criticism, and possible correction a very important element in the process by which one of the most crucial determinations in a young person's life is made."

Lewis Pike, the former senior associate with ETS's Test Assessment and Evaluation Division who had testified for

NYPIRG, initially had been hesitant to testify against ETS. He knew the testing industry had problems but he wanted reform, not dismantling of the industry. "I wanted something reasoned and balanced," he says. Pike saw that NYPIRG was not seeking to dismantle ETS, just to make it more accountable, and he says, "When NYPIRG's Steve Solomon showed me the misinformation being distributed [by ETS] about the bill, it persuaded me to get involved."

Pike admits that he was skeptical NYPIRG could make changes in the testing industry—but it was a well-earned skepticism. He had tried for the last seven of his sixteen years as an ETS associate to get the company to make public his findings that a test taker could benefit from preparation for the test. ETS did not want to release such information because it would suggest that information from previous tests should be available to allow students to prepare. And since the tests are said to measure basic aptitude, ETS's credibility would be undermined if it was proven that studying for the tests could improve test scores.

McLean-Austen says even she and NYPIRG members were skeptical. "At every step of the way we'd say, 'well, we've done a great job, but that is the end of it.' Clearly [the senator] could not have done it without the number of hours put in by NYPIRG. It was too big an issue for us to tackle alone." With the passage of time, the truth-in-testing effort, she says, "is a legend in Albany."

The battle of truth-in-testing was not fought solely in the state of New York. With help in compiling evidence and expert witnesses from the National PIRG staff, PIRGs in California, Massachusetts, and New Jersey have also fought for truth-in-testing laws. McLean-Austen says ETS has, in many cases, implemented provisions of the truth-in-testing law in other states.

The ETS project, like virtually all PIRG projects,

taught many students things their classes never taught them. As Ed Hanley noted, he and other students working on the ETS project learned a whole range of skills as well as an understanding of how those skills are used to promote change. They learned to speak on behalf of NYPIRG's bill before various organizations, and they learned how vital getting the support of those organizations is to successful promotion of a proposal. They learned how to investigate a large corporation, and they saw first hand how important it is to have their case well documented. Students held press conferences and met with reporters and editors; from that they learned about the power of the media and how to present their case to ensure the best coverage.

## VOTER REGISTRATION

Since PIRGs have always emphasized citizen involvement in the political process, it was only natural for them to promote that involvement at its most basic: voting.

So, in the fall of 1983, conferences of the western states' PIRGs and eastern states' PIRGs produced a commitment to a massive nonpartisan voter registration project. The purpose of the project was three-fold: to heighten student interest in the need for voter registration and to train them in voter registration procedures; to reverse the decline in registration and voting among the nation's youth and to help register hundreds of thousands of low-income and minority citizens by working with community voter registration groups; and to encourage people to exercise their right to vote in both primary elections and the 1984 presidential race.

As a springboard for the registration drive, PIRGs enlisted the support of 880 student government presidents and newspaper editors to call for the convening of a nonpartisan National Student Conference on Voter Registration in February 1984 in Cambridge, Massachusetts. With this broad base of support, the conference drew 1,500 students from forty-two states, the largest conference of its kind since the 1960s. The showing was diverse: people active with student government, college newspapers, PIRGs, minority and women's groups, College Republicans, College Democrats, and peace groups. They attended workshops to learn how each state regulates voter registration, how to use the media in a voter registration drive, how to recruit volunteers, how to work with other groups on campus and in the community, and how to "get out the vote." Representatives from most of the national voter registration organizations attended the conference and served as resource people.

With the conference as a catalyst for student involvement in voter registration, the PIRGs established the National Student Campaign for Voter Registration (NSCVR), based in Boston, to coordinate drives on campuses and in communities nationwide. Overall, the campaign worked with students at more than seven hundred schools to help them develop drives or augment existing voter registration and education projects.

Because state laws vary greatly, the NSCVR developed the LEADS Program (Legal Education and Assistance in Defense of Students), for which a group of PIRG lawyers produced a manual called "Overcoming the Obstacles." It gives a state-by-state analysis of voter registration laws. LEADS also helped in cases where the right of students to register as voters was challenged. For example, at Brown University in Providence, Rhode Island, the mayor tried to have Brown students living in dorms purged from the voter lists, saying they were not actually local residents. LEADS lawyers successfully defended the students' right to vote before the Rhode Island Board of Elections.

In states that have "postcard" registration, volunteers set up tables around campus and in the community to sign people up to vote. Where the process required officials of the state to do the registering, PIRGs helped set up those registrars at convenient locations such as campus cafeterias and shopping malls in the community. Also, PIRGs that have canvasses were able to take advantage of the door-to-door contact with the community and help other community residents register to vote.

In the fall, the NSCVR began its voter education project, distributing fact sheets covering the major issues of the presidential campaign and the positions of the candidates. NSCVR declared October 1, 1984, National Student Voter Registration Day. NSCVR was also part of a coalition of groups called the Emergency Mobilization for the Right to Vote, which declared October 4, 1984, National Voter Registration Day. Those dates marked the beginning of a "get out the vote" campaign for the last three weeks before the election. Volunteers staffed phone banks, sent reminder postcards, and passed out voter leaflets urging people to use the vote they had registered for. Kirk Weinert, publications director of NSCVR, said the campaign's main theme was that "promoting democratic participation is the best way to promote the public interest." Weinert said students involved in the project had differing perspectives on a variety of issues. What prompted them to work on the voter registration project, however, was their shared belief that activating citizens to vote is the crucial step in addressing many of the problems plaguing society.

## DEALING WITH LEMONS

It was—and is—a common problem: cars that don't work. As a consumer group, Connecticut PIRG received many calls each month from irate car owners. But what could the group do for owners of these lemons? It did not have the resources—the staff, the time, the money—to help, on an individual basis, these victims of shoddy workmanship and faulty design.

The answer presented itself in the spring of 1982. Buried deep in the pile of issues to be considered by the legislature was a bill to create a so-called Lemon Law. The bill defined, for purposes of the law, the circumstances under which an automobile is unsatisfactory and the consumer is entitled to either adequate repair or a replacement. It also established that the car *manufacturer* was responsible for such repair or replacement, rather than the car dealer. It said that if a car has the same major defect four times while under warranty, or is in the shop for a total of thirty days in the same period, that car is a "lemon," and the car owner has legal recourse. The bill, however, was likely to die in committee; its author and only sponsor was a freshman Democrat from Hartford named John J. Woodcock, who, while energetic, smart, and committed, lacked the back-room power base so often required to get a bill through the legislature.

CONNPIRG adopted the bill as part of its legislative program for that year. With CONNPIRG and Woodcock working closely together, the bill stood a chance.

It was an uphill struggle, as are many PIRG campaigns. Ed Meirzwinski, executive director of CONNPIRG, recalls going to the mat with car dealers over the issue of how the lemon law would affect them: "In the beginning, the dealers thought the lemon law would hurt them—they didn't realize that the purpose of the law was to specifically establish *manufacturer* liability, to put the blame where it belongs—on the people who were making bad cars."

"Historically," notes Meirzwinski, "the *dealer* was liable for a consumer's problems with an automobile."

The lemon law was written because Woodcock became aware of a lawsuit where a man had been in court for eight years with a lemon. That consumer's car had gone through six engines, several transmissions, and other repairs. Through a lawsuit, he finally won a new car. But, he did not win it from its manufacturer, General Motors; he won it from the dealer. The court ruled that there was no contract between the consumer and the manufacturer, so, under existing Connecticut law, the consumer could not take action against the automaker—only against the dealer where a car was purchased.

Dealers assumed the proposed law would extend this arrangement, despite the fact that it "was designed to create the contract between the consumer and manufacturer that the court had ruled did not exist, and to take the onus off the dealers," said Meirzwinski.

The car dealers were a major stumbling block in the campaign. They were able to exercise amazing clout in the legislature, and seemed to have a consistent group of legislators who would vote their line. "We had to get support from both Democrats and Republicans," said Meirzwinski, "or this bill wasn't going anywhere."

So Woodcock spent his time working the legislative aisles, and CONNPIRG spent its time mobilizing the public. Woodcock recalls he was anxious to get Republican support for the lemon law, because "Republicans had traditionally voted with business, but if we could show them how their constituents were complaining, and how they supported the bill, it could strongly influence the passage of the bill."

Organizing the grass-roots support was, of course, a CONNPIRG specialty. Like other PIRGs, its statewide constituency enabled it to draw support from every district. Members surprised even themselves, though, with their own effectiveness—it took only a month for the lemon bill to become the lemon law.

"In many ways, it was a classic campaign," says Meirzwinski. "The group of legislators we were working with was not from either party hierarchy, and support for the bill developed from a grass-roots base."

CONNPIRG developed that base through public education, lobbying, and organizing, and through creative (and effective) use of the media.

Led by two student lobbyists, CONNPIRG testified at public hearings on the bill, got information to members of the General Law Committee—where the bill started out—and began to lobby other key legislators on the bill. When it was passed by the committee, CONNPIRG turned to consumers who had sent complaint letters about their cars and urged them to contact their legislators urging support of the bill.

"Some of these consumers started contacting other automobile owners about the bill, and these owners were in turn writing to their legislators," Meirzwinski recalls. "We decided it was time to do a media event."

The event would turn out to be a coup for CONNPIRG. It generated an outpouring of consumer support for the lemon law, and CONNPIRG's student lobbyists were able to turn that support into an irresistible force that drove the bill through the legislature.

CONNPIRG held a news conference on the front driveway of the capitol. The group gave out free "Lemon-Aid" to reporters, while two owners of lemon cars displayed their cars and photos documenting the extensive problems they had. One of the citizens Woodcock had invited was so angry that he showed up in his airplane! He flew around the capitol towing a huge banner that said, "My '82 Chevy Is the Reason Connecticut Needs the Lemon Law!"

CONNPIRG and citizens supporting the bill then canvassed the halls of the capitol, presenting legislators with the "LemonAid" and a fact sheet on the lemon law.

With the strong press coverage generated by the conference, letters started to pour into the capitol. Legislators from around the state reported being deluged with mail from irate consumers, and many deserted their position against the bill as a result. It coasted through the House. On the day of the vote in the Senate, Senator Michael Morrano, Republican of Greenwich, who had been the principal opponent, gave a speech endorsing the bill. The rest of the Senate followed suit, and with the governor's signature, Connecticut consumers were given protection under the law.

But seeing the bill enacted was not enough. CONNPIRG was anxious to ensure its success as a law. Close monitoring of its implementation followed, and when a problem arose, a new campaign was launched for an amendment, quickly dubbed Lemon Law II.

The original bill, in order to avoid excessive litigation, mandated that consumers first go through the auto manufacturers' arbitration process in an attempt to settle any dispute. To protect consumers from tricky arbitration programs, the bill stipulated that they be in full compliance with the federal Magnusson-Moss Warranty Act, which governs such programs. But after a short time, it became clear that the arbitration programs in Connecticut were not working the way they were supposed to. So CONNPIRG and Woodcock developed an amendment to the law that established a state-run certification process for the manufacturers' arbitration programs. The amendment authorized the Connecticut attorney general to review all arbitration programs, and if they were found to not be in compliance with federal law, consumers could take their complaints to an arbitration program that would be developed by the Connecticut Consumer Protection Department. The amendment further stated that the state program would have the "full force of law" to award compensation, either monetary or in the form of ordering the manufacturer to provide the consumer with a new automobile.

Lemon Law II easily passed both houses of the Connecticut Legislature, providing even more protection for that state's automobile owners.

The Connecticut law, and CONNPIRG's success in passing it, has served as a model for other states, and other PIRGs. Lemon laws are now on the books in New York, California, Ohio, Massachusetts, and thirty-four other states.

## FOUR

# PIRGs in Action: New York PIRG

In a society that often seems full of intractable bureaucrats and countless dead ends, it is hard to find someone who does not feel overwhelmed by its complexity and resigned to the belief that any attempts to change things are futile.

That is unless you walk into the third-floor offices at 9 Murray Street in New York City. The converted loft there houses the main office of the New York Public Interest Research Group. It also houses students and professionals who have no doubt about their ability to bring about change. Looking at NYPIRG's accomplishments, it's not hard to see where the people active in NYPIRG get their confidence. In its fourteen-year history, the group has tackled everything from standardized testing to negligent disposal of toxic wastes. It has issued countless reports, lobbied bills into law, educated consumers on their rights, and trained thousands of students in research, writing, advocacy, and public speaking skills. In short, it has done everything Ralph Nader said students could do through a group like PIRG—and then some.

The office on 9 Murray Street, upon first glance, may seem as unwieldy as the system that students and staff who work there are trying to reform. The walls are covered with posters and press clippings featuring NYPIRG's work, and stacks of studies published by NYPIRG line the rooms. Phones are constantly ringing, and snatches of conversation drift over the low walls of the cubicles that make up the staff's offices: "How late do you think the legislative session will last?" "I have the organizing manual ready for the training conference." "Did you call the press about the campaign-reform conference?" There are some common themes from day to day—training new activists, community education, legislative action—but they encompass a wide range of NYPIRG activity.

Some things—long hours, research, phone calls, writing—are always part of a day's work at NYPIRG. Beyond that, a "day in the life of NYPIRG" can be described in a word: hectic. It isn't unusual for someone to come into the office waving an edition of one of the city's newspapers that has an article on a NYPIRG project. If a NYPIRG bill is supposed to be considered by the legislature, there are frequent calls to Albany to see what progress has been made, and the news is called out to anyone in the office who wants to know. People round up volunteers to make posters for a demonstration on toxic victims, or they have fellow staff members look over a press release. The day wears on, but never seems to wind down. About the time most New Yorkers are taking the subway home, staff working on the Straphangers Campaign are looking at ways to get the city to improve services in the transit system without increasing fares. While people relax at home, turning up their heat or air conditioner, as the case may be, the NYPIRG Fuel Buyers Group is setting up contracts where individuals, banding together, can buy fuel in bulk and save hundreds of dollars each year. Around seven o'clock, volunteers come into the office to staff phone banks. A NYPIRG-endorsed change in the statute of limitations—which could benefit people injured by exposure to hazardous materials—is coming before the Senate for a vote, and the volunteers are urging residents to call their senators to voice their opinion.

Although there is nothing in the bylaws dictating long hours, they are generally par for the course at NYPIRG. They stem mostly from the large amount of work that always needs to be done, but can also be attributed to the camaraderie that pervades the office. A trip to the coffee machine may wind up being a full-fledged discussion of President Reagan's higher education cuts or of the best place in the state to go rock climbing. Throughout the day, people take breaks to talk about what they are doing, to get advice and give encouragement. And for all the energy pumped into NYPIRG projects, there is often still time for an outing, a game of Frisbee, or a movie.

Such diversions may always be a part of working for NYPIRG, but they have had no effect on the quality or quantity of work the organization does. From its beginnings in 1973 with one office, six staff, and little money, NYPIRG has grown into the largest citizen action organization in the state. In 1987, NYPIRG has outposts in virtually every corner of the state from Buffalo and Binghamton to Albany and Stony Brook. NYPIRG has twenty-six offices, twenty campus chapters, seventy-six full-time professional staff, and a yearly budget of $2.5 million.

Each day a steady stream of educational materials, reports, and testimony move off the printing presses; files of NYPIRG canvassers troop out into the community to get support on petitions and raise funds. At the Murray Street office, staff lawyers prepare briefs for NYPIRG's court suits and regulatory interventions, and organizers pore over maps of communities that even the government seems to have forgotten. Down the hall, staff scientists evaluate the results of a NYPIRG study of drinking water or toxic air pollution, and in yet another office editors write press releases and articles for the group's magazine,

*Agenda for Citizen Involvement.* Hundreds of students from twenty campuses take part in NYPIRG projects at their schools or through the legislative internship program in Albany.

Many PIRGs across the country have had a significant impact on their states. Many have passed laws, and won court cases. Many have reached out to inform and influence their local communities. But, except for MASS-PIRG, which is larger, none have grown quite so big, diversified, and effective as the PIRG in New York. Thomas Wathen first got involved with PIRG in 1974 in Indiana. Five years later, he came to NYPIRG. He recalls, "It wasn't until I came to NYPIRG that I had a true idea of what a PIRG could do." Wathen went from seeing what a PIRG could do to serving as NYPIRG's executive director.

All this activity is going on in a state that Donald Ross once said was "unorganizable."

Given the size and diversity of the state, it's no wonder Ross made that observation. Yet he liked a challenge, so he accepted the position of executive director in 1973. But even before he came on board, the organization was taking shape.

In the summer of 1972, Mark Litwak and Jay Hershenson were Queens College juniors, both involved in the strong student government at the college. While attending a national student conference in Washington, D.C., the two heard Ralph Nader give a speech on the PIRG idea and attended the workshop run by two of Nader's staff who were organizing PIRGs on college campuses around the United States. Litwak and Hershenson were intrigued and set out to learn more about PIRGs.

A few months earlier, through a successful referendum, students at Syracuse University in upstate New York had formed a PIRG, which they named Central New York PIRG. Around that time students at the State University of New York at Buffalo had formed what was, in effect, a

*PIRGs in Action: New York PIRG*

PIRG club called Western New York PIRG (WNYPIRG). By the fall, Syracuse had incorporated its PIRG and reached an agreement for funding with the campus board of trustees. Neither school's PIRG, however, had enough money to establish a statewide organization. What was needed, students from both schools realized, was a PIRG chapter on one of the larger state or city college campuses. That would provide more students to work on projects and more funding to make sure the projects could get off the ground. Litwak and Hershenson realized that too.

Hershenson wrote a column for the school paper, *Newsbeat*, to explain the PIRG concept and invite students' involvement. The next week, he was surprised to read a lengthy attack on PIRGs by a member of the group calling itself Young Americans for Freedom (YAF). The YAF article attacked the PIRG funding mechanism as well as the PIRG projects, and it quoted administrators from around the country as opposing PIRGs. Hershenson did some checking and found the article was lifted word for word from a YAF manual, although the author did not make mention of that source. He called the administrators who were mentioned in the article, and they said they weren't contacted for the quotes attributed to them. Armed with these facts, Hershenson exposed the problems in the YAF article by writing his own reply, which ran in parts for three weeks. The heated exchange in print focused campus attention on PIRG—and most of the attention came in the form of support.

In addition to the newspaper articles, Litwak and Hershenson covered the campus with posters, literature, and copies of *Action for a Change*, the PIRG organizing manual. By March, petitioners had compiled nearly twelve thousand signatures. They picked up endorsements from the Student Senate, both student newspapers, and most student organizations. After a session with a skeptical Academic Senate, which needed to be convinced the PIRG fee refunding mechanism was equitable, the group received an endorsement from that senate as well. The petitions allowed the organizing committee to hold a referendum that saw the largest turnout for a student election in the school's history. The PIRG idea was favored 8 to 1 among the voters. The next step was to get approval from the Board of Higher Education, the governing body of City University of New York. With a memo of support from College President Joseph Murphy and the overwhelming show of support from the students, the board approved the funding to begin in the spring of 1973.

The addition of Queens College pumped more than $100,000 a year into the PIRG budget, and students in the scattered schools of Buffalo, Syracuse, and Queens sat down to develop the ties that would bind the campus chapters into an effective statewide organization.

The first step was to write the organization's bylaws and find an executive director. David Fields chaired a nine-hour meeting in which the interim board of directors wrote the bylaws and formed an executive director search committee. After interviewing several candidates, the choice was clear: Donald Ross. A native of the Bronx with a law degree from New York University and three years' experience in organizing PIRGs nationwide, Ross was a natural candidate to head NYPIRG.

Judging from the nature of the first project Ross suggested for NYPIRG, one may have thought he was interested in sinking the group before it even got started. But Ross wanted to put NYPIRG on the map, and he proposed that the group research and publish detailed profiles of the 191 returning members of the New York State Legislature, modeled on the congressional profiles Nader had released in 1972.

The original members of NYPIRG had high ambitions for the organization, but even so, this project seemed a bit out of reach for the fledgling group. Ross soon convinced them it was not, and in a fashion that has become the trademark of NYPIRG activity, students and staff plunged headlong into the mountainous task.

Litwak, just a few months out of college, was put in charge of the project. "I was a psych major in college," he says. "I didn't know much about the legislature." It was just that perspective that gave him an understanding of what the average constituent would want in a profile of a legislator. With other staff members he drew up lengthy questionnaires for the legislators themselves, their former opponents, and community leaders in their districts. NYPIRG then recruited a virtual army of more than two hundred students and volunteers who fanned out across the state for months conducting interviews. Some students spent all day on the phone picking up quotes and opinions. Others wrote and edited profiles. For months, senior staff attorney Nancy Kramer kept track of the laborious progress of the project, noting on a large chart in her office the passage of each profile from the interviewing to the writing to the rewriting stage. Slowly, through long hours of often tedious work, the project inched toward its final columns.

Ross, Litwak, Kramer, and two student interns wrote, rewrote and edited profiles twelve or more hours a day, six days a week, week after week. In 1973 Marilyn Ondrasik—who would become NYPIRG's executive director nine years later—was an intern on the project. She recalls how they worked in shifts around the clock preparing the 191 profiles, each twelve to fourteen pages in length. The drive to complete the project was bolstered because students and staff realized it could make a name for NYPIRG in the community and in the legislature, paving the way for the group's future undertakings.

Through the summer of 1974 the printing presses turned out the profiles. On September 4 the last profile came off the press. "The legislators had no idea what the profiles would be like when we began the project," Ross says. "We weren't perceived as anything particularly significant. . . . But the profiles really changed things."

So the goal was accomplished. Most of the people involved in NYPIRG in the early days will use the phrase "force to be reckoned with" when they describe the way NYPIRG was viewed after putting out the profiles. While the work tested almost to the limit the stamina of students and staff, the profiles provided NYPIRG with a common project for the entire state, and put NYPIRG on the map of the consumer movement in a big way.

## LOBBYING

> A senator meets with a lobbyist. They have lunch. Or dinner. The lobbyist represents John Q. Corporation. He is well dressed and well heeled. He buys the drinks and the meal. He explains the bill he wants the senator to support. He doesn't have to explain that John Q. Corporation donated big bucks to the senator's last campaign. Backs are slapped and bills are passed . . .

That scenario may fit some people's image of lobbying but generally the work has gotten a bit more sophisticated. To be sure, there are some elements that hold true, particularly that the corporate lobbyist can point to his boss's large campaign contribution when presenting legislation to a member of the Senate or Assembly. Wielding that kind of power, it is no surprise that the lobbyists always have legislators' ears, and often have their vote. The NYPIRG lobbying program has little money, and NYPIRG never contributes to candidates. But the organization is wielding another kind of power in the halls of the Albany capitol: grass-roots organization teamed with well-documented presentations.

When NYPIRG waded into the legislative arena, the

group knew it would never have the access to legislators that big-time lobby groups have. But it did know it would have access to the facts surrounding an issue, and access to people in the community who care enough about issues to push their elected representatives to take action. Coordinating those two things would be an important factor in the success of the PIRG's efforts in Albany. "We have the ability to combine very credible research with an ability to mobilize large groups of people to make their opinion known," explains Jay Halfon, NYPIRG's legislative director since 1984. Because of that, this student group, which many legislators thought would dissipate after a short time like so many student efforts, is gearing up for another year as a "force to be reckoned with" in Albany.

Since 1974, NYPIRG has drafted and helped pass a stream of important laws. Much of attorney Kramer's political reform packet—including a freedom-of-information act, an open-meetings law, and a lobbyists' registration law—have been enacted by the legislature. In 1975, NYPIRG persuaded the legislature to change the focus of the state Atomic Energy Commission from promoting just atomic energy to educating the public on all kinds of energy. It became the Energy and Resource Development Agency, now called Energy Research and Development Authority. In 1977, NYPIRG pushed seven bills through the legislature, including a generic drug law, a plain language bill to clarify consumer contracts, and a major marijuana decriminalization act. It has passed a law regulating hearing aid sales practices, and a law giving all New York State taxpayers the right to sue the state over improper expenditures. It has persuaded the legislature to tighten loopholes in the laws governing small claims courts—the so-called people's court—to make it easier for people to collect judgments awarded by those courts.

With the federal government threatening to turn the defunct West Valley nuclear reprocessing plant into a permanent nuclear waste disposal site, NYPIRG in 1979 drafted and successfully promoted a law that bars the opening of such sites without approval of the legislature and governor. NYPIRG was the leading force for passage of truth-in-testing legislation, which forced companies that produce standardized college entrance exams to provide students with more information about the results. In 1982, NYPIRG ran the campaign to pass the bottle bill, a bill that had languished in the legislature for almost a decade.

Most recently, NYPIRG has been working to strengthen state environmental laws. The group won passage in 1986 of a $1.4 billion bond act to speed hazardous-waste cleanup, and it was also successful in its campaign for statute-of-limitations reforms to allow victims of toxic exposure to seek compensation previously denied them. The New York statute of limitations sets the time period after an injury within which a person can seek compensation: three years from the date of exposure. Yet most chemical-induced illness does not occur for more than a decade after exposure, so many victims have no recourse. NYPIRG began working in the 1983 legislative session to get a new statute passed—one that gives victims three years from the date of *discovery* of the cause of injury or illness. Chris Meyer, who helped lobby on the bill in 1985, notes that the laws on the books were made when people were seeking compensation for different kinds of injury. Back then, it was a matter of "when a horse kicked you in the teeth, you knew then what hurt you," Meyer says. Now, he says, today's victims of diseases such as asbestosis contracted the disease decades ago. Women whose mothers used the drug DES during pregnancy may be subject to cervical cancer, but it does not show up until they are in their mid- to late-twenties.

The Toxics Victims Access to Justice campaign sought to allow suits timed to diagnoses, bringing New York in line with other states on this issue. Before four hundred people gathered at a NYPIRG-sponsored toxic victims "lobby day," Governor Cuomo declared in May 1986 that statute-of-limitations reform is one of two top priorities of his legislative agenda. With this backing, NYPIRG was successful in passing the legislation to protect victims' rights.

Another environmental project that has become a NYPIRG priority is full-scale municipal recycling. A new report by the NYPIRG Toxics Project, *The Burning Question*, criticizes a New York City plan to burn municipal trash, and charges that the incineration plan would release tons of toxic gases into the atmosphere around the city. Full-scale recycling, the report says, is a viable option that poses none of the hazards of incineration.

Using the canvassing operation, which has eight offices across the state, and staffing phone banks when bills are coming up for a vote, NYPIRG has more regular contact with people in the districts than most legislators do—not something any politician can take lightly. NYPIRG has also been coming back year after year with reams of research findings and dozens of proposals. "Now we're looked to as a reliable source," Halfon says. "Legislators look to NYPIRG to provide them with the other side of a bill industry is pushing."

Still, NYPIRG is vastly outnumbered by corporate lobbyists. Of more than five hundred lobbyists registered in Albany (known because a NYPIRG bill required them to register), the vast majority represent corporations, banks, and trade associations. There are a few groups working on either consumer or environmental issues, but only NYPIRG works on those issues as well as taxes, banking, and sales fraud, among others. As Halfon points out, if there is a committee hearing on a banking bill, the NYPIRG lobbyist, as the lone consumer representative on that issue, will be "lost in a sea of pin-stripe suits," the numerous banking lobbyists. In addition, whereas Halfon was hired one year out of law school to head NYPIRG's lobbying program, with only a few years' experience with NYPIRG, industry and special interest lobbyists have extensive experience and political clout.

But all this hasn't prevented NYPIRG from being successful in its lobbying. In 1983, the group saw two of its priority proposals advanced by the governor's action. Executive Order #33 required the Department of Environmental Conservation to develop an Industrial Chemical Survey in order to ascertain where companies had disposed of hazardous wastes since 1972, and what chemicals had been disposed of. The so-called right-to-know law has already revealed 449 previously undiscovered dumps or waste sites.

The second issue concerned establishment of a citizens' utility board, by which consumers have formal standing to represent their interests when utilities ask for rate increases, and to monitor utility services. The governor asked the Public Service Commission to implement the CUB administratively. After a series of hearings across the state in 1983 and 1984, the PSC declared that a CUB was needed in New York State, and that it would authorize access to the utility billing envelopes to CUB-like organizations. The utility companies in New York immediately filed suit against the PSC policy, and a lower court ruled recently against CUB. NYPIRG is considering whether to appeal the decision, given the March 1986 U.S. Supreme Court decision against the California Public Utility Commission in a somewhat similar case. Whether or not an appeal is filed, NYPIRG and other utility activists in New York State believe that the New York CUB regulations and authorization differ significantly from the California case, and that CUB, after some modifications, will finally become a reality for New York State utility consumers.

Other recent NYPIRG victories included a law to set

maximum check-clearance delays by banks and a law to create a public transportation safety board, which has the power to investigate traffic accidents.

NYPIRG also plays a role in "red-flagging" bills that would hurt the consumer. For example, in 1983, a bill that would have eliminated the last major restriction on how much money banks could invest out of state was squelched after NYPIRG met with the chairman of the Assembly Banking Committee and argued that banks should be required to invest at certain levels within the state, since they use New Yorkers' money.

Another area NYPIRG is concerned with is lobbyists' accountability. For that reason, the PIRG advocated, and the legislature approved, a commission on lobbying to regulate the profession: monitoring who is lobbying, how much they are spending, the campaign contributions made by the groups they represent, etc. Now, however, the commission is nothing more than a boondoggle. It produces an annual report at a cost of about $300,000 to the taxpayers. If that is all it will do, it should cost less, Halfon says. The commission comes up for reauthorization every two years, and since it is not fulfilling the goals NYPIRG and other consumer groups had in mind when they promoted it, they are now calling for its abolition.

On the other hand, sometimes NYPIRG will favor a weakened version of a bill if that is the only way it will pass that year; then PIRG works in subsequent years to beef it up.

Halfon admits that some legislators do not particularly approve of the way NYPIRG works: "Part of the reason is that we're in the community telling people what they [the legislators] are doing."

Karen Burstein, former state senator and head of the New York Consumer Protection Board, now head of the Civil Service Commission, said, "Some legislators still don't like NYPIRG. They say NYPIRG is too loud, too pushy, that it makes too big a deal of some issues." Burstein adds without hesitation, "That means PIRG is effective."

Of course, the consumers who benefit from NYPIRG's work do not see the group as being too loud or pushy, just persistent. And they do not think the issues PIRG takes on are frivolous.

Evan Pritchard, legislative advisor in Albany for the American Association of Retired Persons, has worked with NYPIRG to lobby some bills of concern to older residents, such as utility reform and hearing aid sales reform. "NYPIRG has done a very good job on a number of bills," he says. "I find it very refreshing to know members of the younger generation are interested in these public issues."

As for students who join the NYPIRG Legislative Program, Halfon says that in the six-month internship "they do all the tasks of professional lobbyists." They draft legislation, present it to the appropriate committee and to legislators who might sponsor it, air the issue in the press, and seek the grass-roots support. When the bill is being considered, they sit through committee hearings and write memos clarifying points of a bill or rebutting opponents' attacks.

"One of the major purposes of PIRG is to train advocates," says Halfon. "Most of students' classroom instruction is geared toward an academic approach to government. But NYPIRG is the only internship in the state for learning how politics work through an advocacy role. People leaving the internship leave with a tremendous amount of education that most college classes don't offer." Not only do students learn a great deal about the legislative process—they learn about substantive issues.

Burstein believes the fact NYPIRG has established a consistent approach while having a regular changeover of people has played an important part in its success. This constituency assures legislators PIRG "isn't a gnat that will go away after a while," she says, and the new people

## PIRGs in Action: New York PIRG

coming in each session provide a renewed vitality to the group's efforts.

"In the eighties, it is considered very bad form to have passion, but there is still that measure of passion among PIRG staff and members," she says. That is what will assure NYPIRG's place in the future of New York lawmaking, if not in the hearts of all lawmakers: "What is terrifying [to legislators or special interest lobbyists] is the notion of selfless passion; you can't buy them off or shut them up," she says. Burstein remembers the NYPIRG lobbyists being tireless, too. "My memory of them is one of people sort of unshaven and exhausted trying to get those last few votes."

But even the people who disagree with NYPIRG will admit the importance of having the "countervailing force" on issues. Dave Schaffer, secretary of the Business Council and former Associated Press reporter in Albany, says, "NYPIRG is extremely effective. It is a well-organized . . . fully professional counterpart." Although the Business Council and NYPIRG both supported criminal penalties for corporate officers who illegally dispose of toxic wastes, they are often "on opposite sides of most issues," Schaffer says. While the PIRG does not have the budget other lobbying groups have, "NYPIRG's basic strength has been the credibility of its arguments rather than its size," he says.

The group's importance in the halls of the capitol was recognized in a recent *Albany Times Union* article: "Call NYPIRG the successor to the groups that trekked to Washington to march against Vietnam or wrote letters to further the cause of civil rights. After ten years, also call NYPIRG one of the pieces needed to complete the jigsaw puzzle picture of New York state government."

And if the plans of NYPIRG students and staff mean anything at all, NYPIRG will be a part of the legislative picture for years to come.

MORE ACTION FOR A CHANGE

## CITIZENS WAKE UP TO THE TOXIC NIGHTMARE

The names of compounds such as dioxin, polychlorinated biphenyls (PCBs) and 2,4,5-T have become frightening additions to many Americans' vocabularies. The federal government bought out the contaminated town of Times Beach, Missouri, because the danger from dioxin was endemic. In Niagara Falls, New York, the community known as Love Canal was torn apart by the discovery of widespread leaking of deadly chemicals, which found their way into peoples' homes and water supply, leaving sickness and many serious ailments in their wake. PCBs have been banned from production, yet they are often discovered uncontained in the environment. The use of herbicides containing 2,4,5-T and its dioxin by-product has been restricted. It is now well known that hundreds of virtually odorless, invisible chemicals can cause far too visible problems for human health and the environment.

But when NYPIRG first began working on the issue of toxics, there was no Love Canal or Times Beach in the news. Americans were becoming more and more aware of the obvious forms of environmental damage such as air pollution, oil spills, and strip mining, but it was 1975 and the menace of chemical pollution was not commonly known. With the lack of public awareness, NYPIRG had a significant task before it when it decided to investigate the problem of toxics in New York. Though preliminary studies, done by government and independent groups, were showing a correlation between cancer and chemicals in drinking water, there were no firm guidelines about what chemicals should be banned from water supplies. There also were many skeptical politicians who needed solid evidence before they would pass laws providing for expensive cleanup of toxics. What's more, any enforcement of regulations would require dedicated monitoring, yet few labs were equipped for the sophisticated, costly analysis required to discover and measure the chemicals.

Such obstacles might have seemed like impasses to many, but not to NYPIRG.

The group decided to get involved in the toxics issue after an Environmental Defense Fund study showed a high correlation between toxic, organic chemicals in drinking water and cancer among those who drank the water. The study, done by Dr. Robert Harris of EDF (who started his drinking water research with Ralph Nader), looked specifically at the problem in the New Orleans drinking water supply, but it was clearly not an isolated case. It pointed to the likelihood of such contamination in communities across the United States. Joseph Highland, a former PIRG organizer working for EDF, suggested to NYPIRG that it examine the problem of toxics in New York.

That's where Walter Hang comes in. The story of NYPIRG's work on toxics is paralleled by Hang's involvement with the organization. He had a degree in biology and had done cancer research in the laboratory, but his background had not prepared him for going before the public, working with government agencies, interpreting federal law, or proposing new regulations. But he was interested in exploring those areas, and going beyond lab work. He once said, "I was in the lab twelve hours a day. I wasn't talking to anyone. I was killing thousands of rats. Finally, I said, 'This is crazy. Why am I doing this and what do I think I'm accomplishing?'" Hang was ready to work in the "real world" and have a direct impact with his work. Likewise, NYPIRG, as an organization, was still fairly new to the public and it certainly was not seen as the authority on chemical pollution. It did not have the high visibility at that point, so its proposals were still met with considerable skepticism. Yet, after ten years, five major studies, national media attention, and several new laws and regulations, Hang and NYPIRG are often turned to as authorities on toxics in the state.

That he would ever be considered an authority on the subject was probably the farthest thing from his mind when the newly hired intern Walter Hang first met with NYPIRG staff. "I was baffled," Hang admits.

Prior to the EDF study, Congress had been considering the Safe Drinking Water Act, and a few weeks after Harris's study on New Orleans water came out, Congress passed the act. It followed on the heels of the Clean Water Act, which regulates the pollutants in industry waste water. The CWA is designed to protect lakes, streams, and other bodies of water from pollution, and the SDWA was set up to make sure that water coming from the tap was free of hazardous chemicals.

However, some things just don't adhere to acts of Congress—chemical pollution is one of those things. While the new law gave government the responsibility for ensuring safe water, it did not provide for specific protection. Congress charged the Environmental Protection Agency with determining what chemicals to regulate under both acts. The lack of comprehensive information on the dangers of many toxics, combined with the lumbering bureaucracy of the EPA, has resulted in only seventeen inorganic chemicals being monitored under the SDWA, in addition to six toxic organic chemicals. One hundred twenty-nine "priority pollutants" are regulated under the Clean Water Act. There are hundreds more that are likely to pose health hazards, but are still not addressed by regulations on the books.

With that broad and as yet undefined framework, Hang's first meeting with the staff on the issue included the unfamiliar "legalese and bureaucratese" that would come into play as regulations were set under the laws.

After the meeting, Hang took NYPIRG staffer Paul Moscovitz aside and said, "I'm a biologist; I don't know anything about the laws." Moscovitz handed him a copy of the Clean Water Act and suggested he read it. It took days for Hang to wade through the language. And that was not all the wading through he would do. Hang, Jay Silberman, and other staff and interns went headlong into an intensive review of all the industries discharging wastes into the Hudson River, until they pinpointed the most heavily contaminated areas and went out and took samples.

Just compiling the data was a fifteen-month process. Since studies of toxics were relatively new, the researchers were not sure where to begin. Their first step was to conduct interviews with officials of the agencies charged with monitoring water standards to find out what records were kept. From there, they pored over hundreds of pages of documents that outlined the compounds discharged by various industries along the Hudson. It was up to NYPIRG to target the compounds that might be toxic and research each specific compound to find out if it was. "I spent endless days in the musty Chemist Club library," Hang says. "I think I was the only person to use the place in ten years," he joked.

Finally, NYPIRG had a list of the industrial plants the group believed were discharging the toxics into the Hudson. The next step was to gather samples. It was November and in some cases collecting the samples entailed trudging through three-foot snow drifts. In one instance, the effluent was discharged from a pipe at the base of a twenty-foot-deep cauldron; Hang remembers spending until two o'clock one freezing morning collecting the necessary five-gallon sample—one pint at a time—by dangling a container on a piece of rope.

A commercial laboratory, an individual scientist, and the staff of the college labs at Stony Brook did the analysis of the water samples. The analysis showed such known and suspected carcinogens as benzene, tetrahydrofuran, PCBs, toluene, dibutylphthalate, and xylene to be present in the industrial and municipal treatment plant wastewater.

The next step was to analyze the data, write the report, and make recommendations. The report urged officials responsible for New Yorkers' safety and health to give their immediate attention to the problems the study revealed. It urged the installation of quality "activated carbon" filters, which would remove most of the toxics from the water before it was used for drinking. Looking toward the future, NYPIRG and the Environmental Defense Fund called for curtailment of toxic discharges at their source.

They set the release date for August. Hang said it seemed as if everyone at NYPIRG had gone on vacation. "It was nonstop in August. The printing office was full of thousands of uncollated copies of the report," Hang says. "At one point I had to learn how to run the printing press myself."

Hang also got a crash course in writing news releases and holding press conferences. The study, called *Troubled Waters: Toxic Chemicals in the Hudson River*, was released on time, and by all standards, Hang and NYPIRG would have to be accorded an "A" for their first effort on toxics. The results of the study were covered in *The New York Times*, numerous newspapers in the Hudson River area, and the wire services. NYPIRG had requests for the study from as far away as Montana, Oklahoma, South Carolina, and Alaska.

The report increased public understanding of toxics and showed politicians that people were concerned. But that was not sufficient to address the problems of toxic pollutants, and NYPIRG was ready to demand more.

"The fire-and-brimstone panic that followed the study fizzled out," Hang says. Public officials merely waited for the attention to the issue to die down some and avoided following through on plans to clean up the water. So, NYPIRG realized it would have to do more studies to show more people were affected. Once people saw that toxics would not go away just because the headlines did, they would bring pressure to bear on government to clean up chemical pollution and to prevent it from happening.

As a follow-up, then, NYPIRG began looking at the problem of toxics in a broader manner.

NYPIRG's next report, using Long Island as a case study, outlined the overall failure of regulation and treatment techniques to address increasing numbers of toxic compounds in drinking water supplies. Next, the investigators did a three-year study of pollution in the Niagara River. They chose the Niagara because it supplies drinking water to 380,000 people. The resulting report, called *The Ravaged River*, found the following:

- There are more than two hundred dumps located in Erie and Niagara counties, with fifty located close to the Niagara River. Yet industry and government had not determined the composition of wastes buried in the sites, or taken action to secure the sites.
- None of the seven water suppliers that tap the Niagara are equipped to cope effectively with potentially hazardous pollutants. The city of Niagara Falls supply system was found to be located adjacent to a massive Hooker Chemical site and less than two hundred yards from a dump where more than seventy-four thousand tons of chemical wastes, including dioxin, were buried.
- Despite mounting evidence about toxic hazards, the study found that regulation of chemicals in

water supplies generally only covers "traditional" concerns such as degradable and visible forms of pollution, ignoring toxic organic chemicals.

These troubling findings attracted the attention of CBS's *60 Minutes*. The following is an excerpt from the segment televised on October 11, 1981.

WALTER HANG: I've looked at seventy-seven permits that have been issued to all the industries along the river, and not one of those permits provides comprehensive controls for organics. As a result, the industries are free to discharge thousands and thousands of pounds of toxic chemicals into the Niagara.

MIKE WALLACE: Mr. Hang, you're calling the roll on some of the biggest chemical names in America—Hooker Chemical, Olin, Carborundum, Union Carbide, DuPont.

HANG: These industries are knowingly discharging vast amounts of toxic chemicals into the Niagara. And worse than that, they're doing it with the blessings of the state and federal environmental agencies.

WALLACE: The *blessings* of?

HANG: When an industry gets a permit, the permit says you are now regulated and you can discharge. But unfortunately, these permits do not place restrictions on the toxic chemicals. So, all these industries are discharging with permits, and yet they are still releasing huge amounts of toxic chemicals. . . . The toxic chemicals that these industries are known to be discharging are among the most toxic chemicals known to science. And they're extremely persistent in the environment. So, day-to-day discharges of toxics accumulate in the river, in the sediment, accumulate in the fish and wildlife that live in the river, and also accumulate in the consumers of the drinking water drawn from the river. So, you're really talking about a long-term hazard that gets more and more serious each and every day.

The *60 Minutes* piece, along with more and more frequent revelations in the news of other kinds of toxic problems, helped to develop the public's interest in the issue, which served as a mandate for NYPIRG to continue its work.

A fourth study looked at a Long Island landfill and found more than a dozen toxic chemicals to be present. Again, regulations, in this case for garbage dumps, have not addressed the problem of toxic chemicals.

NYPIRG was learning that pushing for enforcement of existing rules and regulations would fall short of the goals of cleaning up the environment, for the regulations themselves were inadequate. The group decided that new laws were needed.

In 1981 NYPIRG proposed a legislative remedy to the toxics problem—the state Superfund bill. It would tax generators of hazardous wastes and operators of waste storage sites to create a $10 million fund annually for cleaning up toxic dumps. The bill was passed by the New York State Assembly and sent to the Senate.

NYPIRG's reports had generated a great deal of public concern, so the PIRG sought to channel that concern where it would do some good. Using the door-to-door canvass and phone banks, they advised residents that the Superfund bill was being considered but that it was in danger of being killed in the Senate. In a three-day period, NYPIRG generated one thousand letters from constituents of Senator John R. Dunne, Republican of Garden City, chairman of the Conservation and Recreation Committee, in favor of the Superfund. NYPIRG also worked with other concerned community and environmental groups, and the groundswell led to passage of the Superfund in the previously unfavorable Senate on its last day in session.

But a measure to clean up existing wastes was not all the state needed. From Love Canal to Long Island, it was clear that companies had been dumping a range of toxics for decades. The public has a right to know what is in those dumps, NYPIRG argued. Thus, the organization proposed a "right to know" bill in 1982 to force industries that disposed of hazardous matter in the last thirty years to report the location and content of the dumpsites. When the bill did not pass the legislature, Governor Mario Cuomo, a supporter of the right-to-know concept, issued an executive order instructing the Department of Environmental Conservation to require industry to meet the requirements the law would have established.

And NYPIRG is geared up to make sure the public takes advantage of its right to know. The group continues to document ground water contamination and hazardous landfills, and it is compiling a list of generators, transporters, and disposers of hazardous wastes. NYPIRG is also working with other groups and people in the community to force industry to account for its wastes, to force officials to investigate sites and determine health hazards, and to suggest how Superfund money should be used for cleanup efforts. Students on campuses all over the state are monitoring records to determine whether industries have paid into the state Superfund, and are helping educate the public about how to use the right-to-know regulation and obtain access to industry records. NYPIRG is also seeking changes in the right-to-know program that would make it easier to identify New York's hazardous waste sites and the specific chemicals they contain, and continues to seek additional money for the state Superfund.

Hang is in his eleventh year at NYPIRG. He has seen the organization make great strides in getting the state to address chemical pollution, and in getting the public to recognize the problem and become watchdogs themselves. To be sure, there are still numerous landfills and industrial polluters, and toxic chemicals are still too prevalent in New York. But NYPIRG has sparked the public's concern, and helped open the channels for that concern to be addressed by establishing laws and making citizens aware of their ability to use them. And those are essential elements in reducing the problem of toxic pollution.

## BANKING ON CITIZEN ACTION

Students at Brooklyn College could see it all around them. The neighborhoods were going downhill. People moved out and no one moved back in their place. As the number of abandoned and dilapidated houses grew, so did the crime and fire hazards, but police and fire protection were decidedly deteriorating as well. Sanitation services were declining and that added excessive garbage and rodent problems to the decaying scene.

The students suspected that a bank practice called redlining was a leading factor in the neighborhood decline. Redlining means banks in effect draw a line around a community on the map and refuse to reinvest depositors' money in that neighborhood. Bank redlining usually leads to insurance redlining, as well. As the neighborhood falls into disrepair, people and businesses become reluctant to move in. Lifelong residents reluctantly face the prospect of making an expensive move that takes them away from their friends and perhaps farther from their jobs.

The Brooklyn College NYPIRG students wanted to

determine the extent of local redlining. A team of students sifted through the records in the Brooklyn Municipal Building. First, they pored over ledgers that contained the basic information on all home mortgages granted in the borough, carefully noting the bank granting the mortgage, the property owner, the block and lot designating the property location, and the volume number directing them to the next set of records they needed. There they found the value of the mortgage and street address of the home that received it.

For five months, the students spent hundreds of hours studying these records, eventually looking at the mortgage figures for each of the more than *nine thousand* blocks in the borough.

When they had finished compiling the mortgage records they turned to the banks themselves. From annual reports they determined the total assets, total deposits, overall mortgage investment, annual mortgage investment, and the number of branch offices of each of seven Brooklyn banks chosen for the survey.

On December 6, 1976, they released the results of their investigation, aptly titled *Take the Money and Run*.

What the students found was that six of the seven banks were taking the dollars deposited by Brooklyn residents and investing the money somewhere else—anywhere else—but not back in Brooklyn. Only one of the seven invested any reasonable percentage of its assets in Brooklyn. And all seven banks granted virtually no mortgages in black and Hispanic neighborhoods. In all, the seven banks with assets of almost $11 billion had issued only $40 million in mortgages on Brooklyn properties in 1975.

So while Brooklyn residents were unable to get a mortgage, their money and that of their neighbors was being shipped out of Brooklyn and even out of the state. While the neighborhoods in which they operated were decaying, the bankers were protesting that their only responsibility was to keep secure the interest rate they paid to depositors. Next, it was the residents' turn to protest. Once the credit is entirely cut off, the community is locked into the poverty cycle; the people of East Flatbush did not want to sink into that cycle. Many of them had lived in their neighborhood all their lives, and they did not want to flee the community and allow it to die. Many could not afford to leave either. So they decided to stand and fight.

It was December 7, one day after the release of the students' report on redlining, that Marilyn Ondrasik found herself standing in front of one hundred or more East Flatbush residents crowded into a small neighborhood church. The residents had gathered to address the redlining problem. Ondrasik was prepared to help them. In the summer of 1976, she had taken a leave of absence and attended an organizing program run by John Gardner of the United Farmworkers in St. Louis. There she learned about localized grass-roots organizing, and in the fall of 1976, back in New York, Ondrasik began applying the new method of organizing. People she spoke to were all too aware that the neighborhood was declining, but many of them attributed it to changes in the racial mix; that reasoning kept them from seeing the control the banks were exercising. Many of them were not familiar with the idea of redlining, either. Ondrasik remembers that some thought she was saying "redlighting," and they would ask: "Doesn't that have something to do with prostitution?"

But now the word was out about redlining. The residents filled the local church to capacity, and Ondrasik began to tell them case studies of families who had been redlined. It was not long before the people she mentioned jumped up and told the stories themselves. Soon she sat down and turned the meeting over to the audience. They exchanged stories of being refused mortgages and home improvement loans, and it became apparent that the banks were the culprits. One man said that "not even God himself could get a loan in Brooklyn." Ondrasik asked them if they were ready to do something about that. They were. They formed the first Bank on Brooklyn (BOB) chapter and launched NYPIRG's first community reinvestment campaign. Says one resident who got involved in the campaign: "We were real concerned about the things happening [to our neighborhood], and finally someone was able to point to the source of the problem and tell us how to solve it."

One of their first targets was the Flatbush Federal Savings and Loan. The bank had recently invested in a large sign proclaiming "New York City—We Love You." In Ondrasik's opinion, it was about their only investment in the city. While hundreds of millions of dollars were being sent out of New York, Ondrasik remembers, the bank had only put down a few hundred thousand dollars in area mortgages.

At first the bank simply refused to meet with Ondrasik and the BOB activists. So in the bitter cold of February and March 1977, about sixty residents picketed their East Flatbush branch on Mondays and Fridays. They began to pass out petitions and pledge cards outside the bank, the pledgers affirming that they would greenline the bank—withdraw their deposits from the bank because of its redlining. "A local church even called up and said they were thinking about withdrawing their money," Ondrasik says. In six weeks, the bank capitulated. It signed an "affirmative action" agreement with BOB and pledged to reinvest $4 million annually in the community and offer mortgages at reasonable terms.

Since then the BOB organizers have signed ten other agreements for a total of $56 million in reinvestment quotas annually. One bank, the largest in Brooklyn, was reluctant to give BOB anything in writing. So BOB members paraded along the Brooklyn Bridge with signs asking drivers to honk if they wanted redlining to stop. "We were everywhere," Ondrasik recalls. The attention BOB gave the issue brought public pressure to bear on the bank regulation agencies, such as the Federal Deposit Insurance Corporation and the New York State Banking Department, and they did respond, at least to some extent. When BOB protested banks trying to open branch offices without serving the credit needs of their local communities, the agencies delayed approval for the branches and in one case denied it.

NYPIRG has launched additional community reinvestment programs in two other boroughs of New York City (the Bronx and Queens), and in Buffalo, Binghamton, and Albany. Teams made up of staff and students have prepared reports on bank redlining in several communities, investigated the State Banking Department's record on regulating redlining, and offered groundbreaking research on the related problem of insurance redlining. And NYPIRG successfully pressed the banking department to adopt the tougher regulations of the Federal Community Reinvestment Act as their own.

But besides persuading bankers and legislators to act on the problem, NYPIRG has done something else too. It has convinced the people who live in these communities that they can stand up and change the course of their own lives. "People use this experience over and over again," says Ondrasik. "When we first began, people were scared to go into banks without an appointment. Then, later, they started to say, 'They won't give us a what?' and go on in without one."

And they have begun to take the lessons of the redlining campaign beyond the banks. Diane and Tom Moogan were a young couple without any real interest in politics when Ondrasik organized the East Flatbush Bank on Brooklyn chapter. Soon they were heading up the campaign as co-chairs of the steering committee. Once the major steps were successfully taken on the redlining issue, they turned their attention to the inadequate sanitation pick-up on the commercial strip near where they live. They used the same community organizing approach that Ondrasik had used. They succeeded in bringing one hundred fifty people into a church for the first meeting of the St. Jerome's Community Action Committee. In a few days, the trucks were on the streets and the garbage was gone. Diane Moogan says their successful organizing could not have been done if they had not learned from NYPIRG how to research and present issues so that others will get involved. The Moogans also realized that no problem is too big—"The ways we learned from NYPIRG to tackle problems are so effective that I will never look passively at problems," Diane says. "Not too many things seem impossible anymore."

The redline work has fostered that change in attitudes in others, too. Ondrasik remembers a shy Cuban woman who barely spoke any English but was always around to pass out pledge cards and get signatures on petitions. The woman lived with her children on a block riddled with junkies and drug dealers. The police were nowhere to be found. So one day the woman walked into the local police station and told them, "I'm with Bank on Brooklyn, you know, the people who picket. Do you want me and my neighbors picketing you twice a week for six months?" The police increased patrols shortly thereafter.

For NYPIRG, too, the redlining effort meant changes. It was by far the most extensive grass-roots organizing the group had ever undertaken, bringing the organization to communities far outside the campus. And it has given NYPIRG a community presence that few even dreamed the organization would ever have.

*PIRGs in Action: New York PIRG*

## ACID RAIN

While the redlining campaign made NYPIRG a household word in several boroughs, its other projects have done the same for the group in communities all over the state and, in some cases, in other states as well.

In 1982, NYPIRG, in a first-time joint effort with Ontario PIRG in Canada, took a unique tour around parts of Canada, New York, and other New England states to call attention to the problem of "acid rain." Acid rain is the product of excessive sulphur in the air; it kills aquatic life and vegetation, contaminates drinking water sources, and causes long-term damage to buildings. Since executives of coal-powered electric generating plants and other industries that spew out sulphur emissions believe cleaning the emissions would be costly, they have exerted their political power to prevent stringent regulation of the amount of sulphur that can be released.

Loading NYPIRG's converted school bus with stacks of literature, banners, sleeping bags, one bicycle, and a guitar, six students and staff from New York and Canada set out on a two-month "Acid Rain Caravan." They stopped at forty cities and towns in New York, New Hampshire, Vermont, Maine, Massachusetts, and Connecticut, and in Canadian cities including Montreal, Ottawa, and Quebec. Their goal was to urge citizens in these hardest-hit areas to pressure their representatives to take action. The timing was ideal: The U.S. Congress was considering the reauthorization of the Clean Air Act; United States and Canadian groups were seeking to get "acid rain" amendments that would place restrictions on sulphur emissions; and Canada-United States negotiations on a Long Range Transport of Air Pollutants treaty had all but collapsed just weeks before the caravan set out for Toronto. These events gave an urgency to the caravan's message; people realized their actions might mean more, coming at such a crucial time.

To prepare for the caravan, organizers gathered literature, displays, and slide shows explaining the issue, contacted people in each community who would help set up meetings with public officials and local groups, and sent out advance press information, which generated seven radio interviews before they even set out, and also gave enough notice so local media would be ready to cover them.

When they came into town, they set up an information table and display board next to the bus. The routine varied some each time, but it usually involved meeting with the mayor or other public official in front of the press, where the caravan would present "acid rain umbrellas" as a symbol of the protection an area needs from acid rain, giving film presentations or talks before local groups, and distributing information from the bus. Mayors in Burlington, Vermont, and Saratoga, New York, proclaimed a "Stop Acid Rain Day" when the caravan visited. On one of the few rainy days during the caravan, the students were able to use a pH meter donated for the summer by the University of Toronto Botany Department. During a press conference with the late New Hampshire Governor Hugh Gallen, the downpour measured a pH of 3.5—which is 125 times as acidic as clean rain.

Measuring the public and official response to the caravan was more difficult than measuring the acidity of the rain. However, the day after the caravan came through his district, Congressman David O'B. Martin, from upstate New York's 30th District, announced his support for the acid rain amendments for the first time. The caravan received extensive publicity, and students were able to talk to thousands of people personally at the information tables and at presentations, so awareness of the issue was heightened.

## PROPERTY TAX

In another wide-ranging project, staff attorney Gene Russianoff was helping the city dwellers get a better chance to appeal unfair property tax assessments.

The action started after NYPIRG research showed that cities were overassessing some dwellings for property taxes, and that the poor and minorities were hit hardest, often paying more than the wealthy homeowners. On campuses in Albany, Long Island, Buffalo, Binghamton, and New York City, hundreds of students were involved in researching property tax structures and avenues for appealing assessments, analyzing the data, and writing reports.

In New York City alone, studies of more than half a million homeowners showed that two hundred thousand were overassessed. The city of New York did eventually reform property taxes, reducing assessments in low-income and minority neighborhoods, resulting in savings as large as $200 for some residents. In a press conference announcing the reductions, New York City Finance Commissioner Philip Michael acknowledged it targeted the neighborhoods because of the NYPIRG reports. Michael introduced Gene Russianoff and NYPIRG's tax reform director, Frank Domurad, saying, "These gentlemen are from NYPIRG. They have been supplying the Finance Department with reliable information we have been using to target neighborhoods for assessment reductions." When Michael's staff had trouble answering a reporter's question about which areas had received the most reductions, Michael asked, "Gene, which are the neighborhoods you asked us to target?"

Another problem with the tax structure was that citizens who wanted to appeal the amount their property was taxed had to go to the city Tax Commission, the same body that set the taxes in the first place. In 1981, of 4,944 private homeowners who appealed assessments, only 1,062 won, and the city granted most of those changes for reasons other than overvaluation. NYPIRG led a successful campaign for a law that would allow owner-occupants of one-, two-, and three-family homes to sue New York City in small claims court, if they have exhausted all avenues of administrative appeal.

New York students are giving a vital image to the word "citizenship." Admittedly, though, most people do not walk into a NYPIRG office saying, "I want to change the boring image that being a responsible citizen has received." They walk in because they are concerned about a particular issue, because they are confronted by a bad product or irresponsible merchant and they want to take action, because they are interested in a project they hear NYPIRG is working on—or because they like the kind of people they see working for NYPIRG. Jesse Schaffer, chairman of the state board in 1982–83, jokes that at Binghamton, a few people are even recruited as they leave the campus pub situated above NYPIRG's office.

Once students do get interested in working with the PIRG, there is usually very little lag time before they are taking on projects themselves. Students may come into the office one day, start working on a market survey the next week, and two months later, see the results—and maybe even their name—in the local paper. Then they are caught in the organization's momentum. As Schaffer says, "NYPIRG always challenges you, it always gives you one more thing to do." Then, he adds, "After a point you realize you're also in the process of learning . . . and gaining skills that you will always use in this society." And that may be when the typical NYPIRG member realizes he or she is a part of something important.

Loretta Simon, who served as statewide campus coordinator, says that NYPIRG appeals to the average student who asks, "How can I make a difference?" The answer is simple, she says. "First, you have to care about the issues, you have to be angered about problems in society. If you have that first ingredient, you've got the second—that's NYPIRG," she explains. "It is the tool to get things done."

F I V E

# PIRGs in Action: Colorado PIRG

A member of the University of Colorado Board of Regents once said he wished students would "be good kids and just drink Coors beer and study." He did not want them to rock the boat.

Colorado PIRG members may not be good in his view, but they are effective—effective at organizing other students and the community; effective at studying problems in the state, from hazardous wastes to utility reform; effective at bringing pressure to bear on public officials to address those problems.

COPIRG was established in 1973 to do what all PIRGs do: investigate problems, then come up with solutions and advocate them. But in Colorado, this course of action has been particularly disagreeable to some officials, so the PIRG has been fighting not only for consumer protection and social reform, but for its survival as well.

The first PIRG organizing drive in Colorado was started by James Kurtz-Phelan, then working as a staff attorney with the University of Denver Clinical Education Program. Kurtz-Phelan had worked with Ralph Nader's Citizen Action Group while in Yale Law School, and in 1970 he authored "The Corporate State," a study of the

*PIRGs in Action: Colorado PIRG*

Du Pont family's wide-ranging influence in the state of Delaware.

Although many Colorado students were enthusiastic, the initial petition drive at the University of Denver was not a success. Only 40 percent of them supported a mandatory fee (COPIRG needed at least 50 percent to institute the fee), and administrators would not allow COPIRG to collect a voluntary fee at tuition payment time.

Kurtz-Phelan had been joined by a 1971 graduate of Colorado College, Jon Frizzell, in the organizing attempt. Frizzel had volunteered for the George McGovern presidential bid and Pat Schroeder's congressional campaign, and that fall he worked for COPIRG as executive director—full-time, without pay, working at odd jobs to pay his bills.

In a renewed organizing effort, Frizzell and Kurtz-Phelan traveled to campuses all over the state, setting up petition drives and building support among students. They also set up COPIRG's first project, chosen because it affected a lot of students and could be done within the PIRG's limited resources.

Kurtz-Phelan explains that students had been telling COPIRG about being "ripped-off" by apartment locator services. For a fee, the agencies were supposed to find a rental unit suited to the customer's needs. What COPIRG members discovered when they posed as customers was that the agencies sent them to places that had been rented weeks before, or to addresses that were vacant lots. COPIRG turned the information over to the Real Estate Commission so it could monitor the situation, and the PIRG helped formulate legislation that would address the problems their study uncovered. COPIRG testified before legislative committees, and within six months of beginning the project, the legislature passed the rental agency reform law, which made the agencies accountable to the state Real Estate Commission.

The project's visibility in its early stages fueled the organizing drive, and in May 1973, after two weeks of petitioning, 500 of the 650 students at Loretto Heights College had signed on in support of COPIRG. When students paid tuition the following September, an overwhelming percentage of students contributed to the first campus chapter of COPIRG.

Successful petition drives were carried out that spring at Regis College in Denver, University of Colorado in Boulder, and Metropolitan State College in Denver. Yet, funding was not approved on those campuses: At Regis, summer break interrupted the organizing drive; at CU, the regents had called a student fee moratorium while they examined a new assessment policy. And at Metro State, administrators argued that colleges could not collect money for a "political organization." Metro State and Denver Community College joined COPIRG a year later with funding from student government allocations, and UC at Denver was granted a neutral check-off that year.

At the University of Northern Colorado, COPIRG organizers collected enough signatures, but were faced with similar opposition from some administrators. The president of UNC, who told *The Denver Post*, "I've supported the notion of COPIRG since I first heard of it," offered an alternative funding method—a positive check-off on the students' registration form. UNC COPIRG accepted the compromise, and five thousand of nine thousand students elected to pay the fee when it was first established.

Even in those early stages, student volunteers began other projects. Kurtz-Phelan recalls, "Students were doing the nitty-gritty work [organizing] on campus and doing research at the same time." One project led to a crackdown on violations of federal regulations requiring flammability labels on children's sleepwear after a COPIRG survey found unlabeled, flammable sleepwear on the shelves of thirty-six department stores in the Denver area. COPIRG burned a pair of child's pajamas at a press conference to illustrate the findings. The project received coverage in the news and favorable editorials.

Another project surveyed sixty-seven pharmacies in Greeley, Fort Collins, Boulder, and Denver. It uncovered prices that varied as much as 400 percent for the same prescription drugs.

In the 1975–76 school year, COPIRG received a boost when Colorado State University at Fort Collins, with its twenty thousand students, approved a mandatory refundable fee. With the additional money, COPIRG began hiring paid staff and carrying out more projects. It did major studies on truth-in-lending by federally chartered banks, sex discrimination by employment agencies, auto repair fraud, and toy safety. It also sued the Environmental Protection Agency to force it to be responsible for regulating radioactive waste water. While the Atomic Energy Commission (now the Nuclear Regulatory Commission) was charged with such regulation, COPIRG believed the EPA could provide more efficient, stricter monitoring, which would provide more protection for Coloradans. The case went to the state's Supreme Court, and though COPIRG lost, media coverage of the case brought the problem of radioactive waste water to the attention of the public.

In the following year, the PIRG met with some problems, both external and internal. Although the group lacked cohesiveness among the chapters statewide, COPIRG went forward with two initiatives on the November ballot—one to reform the Public Utilities Commission and one on a container deposit law. After getting enough signatures over the summer to get the issues on the ballot, the PIRG faced opponents with well-funded war chests on both issues. On the utility commission reform measure, COPIRG's $20,000 expenditures was outmatched 50 to 1 by utility companies. Bottle bill opponents spent similarly large amounts. Without unity among all chapters, the PIRG could not meet the challenge on both fronts. Both initiatives were soundly defeated. COPIRG did get a lot of visibility and student involvement because of the initiatives, but the loss was a blow to the organization.

The loss of morale that followed the defeat was compounded by an attack on PIRG at Fort Collins by a group of opposing students. They succeeded in altering COPIRG's funding process at the state university. The University of Colorado gave COPIRG funding, but it was strictly limited by the regents to on-campus projects. By February of 1977, with the variety of funding methods and spending restrictions in effect for the PIRG chapters, the state board was dismantled. The statewide presence that was the key to PIRG success had dissolved, and so did four campus chapters.

The setback did not last long. By 1979, students on the campuses of University of Northern Colorado at Greeley and Colorado University at Boulder began reorganizing COPIRG, with the help of former Minnesota PIRG Director Jon Motl.

At UNC-Greeley, students sought to upgrade funding to a mandatory-refundable fee. They ran a petition drive and with 51 percent of the students signing, they went to the board of trustees. They pointed to the opportunity and influence students have at strongly funded PIRGs such as Minnesota and New York. Students in Colorado should have the opportunity to become effective as citizens, too, they argued. The trustees agreed.

In the same way, COPIRG was approved at CU-Boulder.

Lest it all sound easy, Motl and other organizers are quick to point out that it is not. "Students should expect to put as much into the organizing drive as they would into organic chemistry or any other demanding course," Motl says. C. B. Pearson, who became a COPIRG organizer in 1979, adds, "It is a long, grueling, sophisticated process to start a new PIRG." And with the absence on several Colorado campuses for almost two years, many students familiar with the group were gone—"We had to reeducate the whole campus about PIRG," Pearson notes.

This was true when the reorganizing drive began at Colorado State University in Fort Collins in 1980. Students set up tables to inform the campus about PIRG. Ann Moorman, then a student at CSU, had heard of COPIRG; her brother Tim was state board chairperson in 1975. Therefore, the group's table caught her eye as she walked through the area known on campus as the "flea market," where organizations typically distribute information. Before long, Moorman was immersed in the organizing drive with other students, speaking before classes and other student groups, petitioning, helping run the referendum, and eventually negotiating with the State Board of Agriculture and the administration for a funding system. The process took six months, but "it was a picture-perfect organizing drive," Moorman says. The board accepted the students' vote in favor of a refundable fee, and CSU became the third strongly funded chapter of COPIRG.

With funding, new visibility, full-time staff, and an influx of student volunteers, COPIRG was able to take on significant projects in the community and in the legislature once again.

## HAZARDOUS WASTES

One of COPIRG's major initiatives has been addressing the problem of toxics in the state.

It is ironic that a state with this political environment—the state that brought us the notoriously antienvironment Secretary of the Interior James G. Watt and EPA

Administrator Anne Gorsuch Burford—has also become the testing ground for some important initiatives to guard against environmental damage. But, because the state is renowned for its pristine slopes for snowskiing, rugged hiking in the Rocky Mountains, and natural rock formations with names like "Garden of the Gods," it made sense for COPIRG to set as a priority protecting those resources and the state's citizens from the danger of hazardous wastes.

Like many states, Colorado has been left with a legacy of "orphan" waste dump sites. For years, generators of a variety of wastes have been able to dispose of the materials with little or no regulation from the state. Now there are thirty-six hundred "surface impoundments," which include ponds, lagoons, and landfills, and three hundred active and inactive hazardous waste sites. A number of the sites are abandoned, and the state Department of Health has estimated that 90 percent of those sites pose a potential health hazard. "It is reasonable to expect that 37 percent of the thirty-six hundred impoundments in Colorado pose an actual threat of contamination to ground water supplies, and that more than 53 percent of the thirty-six hundred impoundments pose a potential threat of such contamination," Robert Arnott, assistant director of the Department of Health, said.

The community of Love Canal, New York, which found high cancer and birth defect rates among people who lived near the abandoned Hooker Chemical Company dump site, provides just one grim example of what can happen if hazardous wastes are not discovered and contained. Dump sites need to be secured to protect citizens' health, and laws are needed to prevent irresponsible dumping.

That's where COPIRG came in. When the legislature began considering amendments to the state hazardous waste policy in 1983, COPIRG got in on the ground floor.

## PIRGs in Action: Colorado PIRG

As a result, legislation has been passed that allows the state to set tough standards for disposal and treatment of toxic and other hazardous wastes.

Geoff Wilson, then legislative director for COPIRG, explains that the legislature was seeking in 1983 to add several amendments to a hazardous waste policy act enacted in 1981. And COPIRG had some ideas about how the policy should be amended. The hazardous waste bill of 1981 didn't allow the state to make any rules that were more stringent than federal hazardous waste regulation. In many cases, federal regulations were woefully inadequate, and COPIRG believed the state should not limit itself to such standards. To illustrate this, COPIRG pointed out one of the more obvious loopholes in an Environmental Protection Agency regulation, called the "small quantity generator exemption." It allows operators who generate less than twenty-two hundred pounds of hazardous materials each month to dump it into landfills designed for solid waste disposal. The rule does not limit the number of "small quantity generators" who can each unload twenty-two hundred pounds in any one dump each month. Therefore, the state could have, say, five generators, each dumping the alloted twenty-two hundred pounds into a site each month. The flaws in such a proposition are numerous, and the dangers posed by filling a site with tons of toxic wastes, when it is not equipped to handle hazardous materials at all, are quite significant.

While such loopholes in the law have a devastating impact, they are usually difficult to ferret out. But COPIRG sifted through the regulations and even discovered other examples of weak "regs." Then they presented the evidence to the legislature. Though COPIRG was new to the lobbying scene, both Republicans and Democrats embraced its argument that "the state ought to be able to be as tough as it needs to be to protect Coloradans' health."

COPIRG also looked to the future. The operators of hazardous waste facilities should not escape accountability as easily as they had in the past. Part of the solution was to amend the act that forced the state- and county-level authorities to consider three criteria when approving land use permits for hazardous waste facility operators in Colorado. The criteria COPIRG proposed, which the state adopted, are:

- The track record of operators coming to Colorado from other states must be reviewed for violation of regulations.
- Facility operators proposing a site must demonstrate a need for a new facility.
- The operator must have the financial ability to pay for a cleanup and for other damages caused in the event of an accident.

Wilson explains that the amendments do not dictate how local officials respond to such information, only that they take it into consideration. It will be left to their discretion whether information about an operator, such as a history of violations in another state, should disqualify that operator from opening a facility in Colorado.

Joan Sowinski, hazardous waste section chief of the Colorado Department of Health, said her office supports COPIRG's work in this area. "Looking at an operator's record is important. If a company cannot show financial stability, it would be prudent to turn them down [for a land use permit]," Sowinski said.

"Finally, the burden of proof is on the operator to show a need for the facility and to show it can be financially responsible for any damages," Wilson says.

Getting the state to enact strong hazardous waste laws

was made easier because of the generally heightened awareness of the problem. But still, it required quality research to document the extent of the problem and to propose solutions. The solutions offered through the hazardous waste act are only the beginning for COPIRG.

Only 9 of the 3,600 Colorado sites were listed on the EPA's original priority list—sites on this list are being considered for federal Superfund money. The Superfund was established by Congress to provide for cleanup of the nation's most hazardous waste sites; 418 had been selected for the list nationwide. There are still 3,591 sites in Colorado, along with whatever hazardous materials they may contain, on the state's hands.

To address the huge gap between the few Colorado sites that are eligible for cleanup under the federal Superfund and the rest of the sites in the state, COPIRG conducted a campaign for a state Superfund, similar to ones already in place in New York and other states.

The new Superfund law, which passed the Colorado legislature in 1985, was the first major environmental legislation introduced by a coalition of groups, including COPIRG, to make its way onto the books. The law imposes a fee on the disposal of all *solid* waste, not just hazardous waste (fifteen cents per cubic yard for commercial users). The immediate aim of the law is to raise the 10 percent of the estimated cleanup costs required to receive federal Superfund money for the Colorado sites on the National Priority List. Ultimately, COPIRG hopes, revenue for cleaning up all the state's sites will be generated through the law.

## RENTERS' RIGHTS

A Denver man had sewage backing up into his bathtub—he could not use the bathroom facilities for a month. Doors were nailed shut in his apartment, so that there was only one working exit. His landlord would not make repairs.

Another renter, a professional businessman with two young children, reported to his landlord that his furnace had a dangerous gas leak. The landlord's response was, "Open the windows." When the tenant complained that there was no heat in the house and that pipes leaking water onto electrical switches and outlets were creating a fire hazard, the landlord had no response at all.

Landlords are in an enviable position in Colorado. In most cases if they choose not to fix a problem, the tenants have no effective recourse short of moving. And with housing vacancies in metropolitan areas of the state hovering at a slim 1 percent, that option is not readily available to tenants. Even if it were an option, under current Colorado law a tenant remains obliged to pay rent for the entire term of the lease despite unrepaired problems. Moreover, making a move can be costly, and can leave residents far from schools and workplaces. And what's more, the next landlord can be just as negligent about maintaining a habitable house or apartment. Nearly one million Colorado residents, thousands of whom are students, rent their homes; yet, there is no statewide law in Colorado requiring landlords to provide even the basics of heat, electricity, and water to tenants.

Citizens' groups have been trying for years to get the legislature to pass a "warranty of habitability law," which would guarantee that rental property is equipped with those necessities, and would force landlords to repair dangerous problems such as gas leaks or faulty wiring. Colorado is one of eight states that does not provide renters with that guarantee. Year after year, the bill has been stalled in various committees—it only came to a vote in the statehouse one time in twenty years but failed to pass both houses.

Sister Lorretta Anne Madden of the Colorado Catholic

## PIRGs in Action: Colorado PIRG

Conference has been working on tenant rights reform for the past ten years, and she says she has been to virtually every committee hearing on the subject during that time. Madden estimates that generally 90 percent of the testimony at these hearings has been from supporters of a warranty-of-habitability law, but "a few get up from the Apartment Owners Association and testify against it and it doesn't pass." The Apartment Owners Association, led by the state's powerful lobbyist Freda Poundstone, says a law to protect renters is unnecessary.

In 1983 COPIRG was able to crack the opposition to warranty of habitability and get the entire state House of Representatives to vote on the bill. Unfortunately the bill lost by one vote.

Madden says COPIRG's well-prepared testimony, along with its effort to coordinate other groups' work on the issue, can be credited with the bill's getting as far as it did.

While a warranty-of-habitability law is not yet on the books in Colorado, Annette Talbot, who coordinated COPIRG's work on the bill, says the effort was "a victory for students. It renewed the faith of all the groups working on [the bill] that we could come this far," Talbot says. "Other groups who had been pushing for the bill had been trying so long they had gotten skeptical," Talbot says.

Talbot saw that skepticism firsthand when she began organizing the coalition. "It took some convincing to get the groups to see that a coalition could have an impact," Talbot says. Her most convincing argument was made when COPIRG held a press conference to explain the problems renters face and the lack of landlord accountability. After three major television stations and numerous newspapers amplified the message presented at the press conference, Talbot says members of the other groups "realized that with good organization, we could have an impact."

The warranty-of-habitability bill, sponsored by Senator Martha Ezzard, Republican of Englewood, and Representative Bill Artist, Republican of Greeley, defines habitable as "maintaining in safe working order and condition all electrical, plumbing, sanitary and heating facilities." In addition, repairs are required on structural defects that would constitute "a substantial threat to the life, health and safety of the occupants." The bill gives the landlord fourteen days to make repairs on conditions that fit those categories. If the repairs are not made, the tenant may terminate the lease without penalty and/or file suit. In addition, tenants are protected from landlord retaliation such as increases in rent, decreases in service, or eviction.

The bill also protects the landlord. A tenant bringing "frivolous action" (one without any basis) must pay the landlord's attorney fees and court costs. A prior-notice clause gives landlords a defense to complaints filed about a situation tenants were informed of before moving in. This clause ensures the warranty would not be used to force upgrading of dwellings such as mountain cabins that are not intended to have the amenities one would expect in a permanent home.

In order to demonstrate the extent of the problem in Colorado, renters testified about defects the landlord was not obligated by law to repair. Renters from a variety of backgrounds, from low-income wage earners to middle-income professionals, participated.

Madden says finding renters who are having problems is easy—each time she speaks to community groups about the issue, she hears several examples of people living without heat, hot water, or sanitary conditions who cannot get the landlord to make repairs, and who cannot afford to move out.

Opponents of the bill argue that local housing codes adequately address the issue. While these codes are useful supplements to a statewide measure, Talbot points out that their effectiveness depends on the resources counties or cities have to enforce the codes. One great advantage of a warranty-of-habitability law is that individuals can take their case to small claims court, which does not require an attorney or government agency action.

The skepticism about COPIRG, as a relatively "new kid on the block," began to fade as the group presented facts, figures, and personal testimony on the issue. Even so, Talbot knows there is still the powerful Apartment Owners Association to contend with before a warranty-of-habitability law will be passed. As Talbot notes, "Opponents say, 'Political reality says you will never get the bill passed.' We say, 'Well, then political reality needs to change.'" A governor's task force on Public/Private Housing Strategies notes the need for change in its report. Franklin James, author of the report, says, "With a tighter housing market, landlords have more and more power; tenants have less and less." The task force, made up of representatives from the housing industry and local and state government, recommends, among other remedies, that the warranty-of-habitability law be passed.

Yet, COPIRG and renters throughout Colorado still have little recourse for unhabitable dwellings. The Denver City Council recently refused to enact a local warranty-of-habitability law, and the state bill remains in committee. It has been reintroduced in the 1987 session, but the chances for securing minimal tenant protections via its passage remain slim.

## CHALLENGES FROM THE RIGHT

The work of COPIRG, like that of all public interest groups, is carried on with great difficulty. Partisan interests are formidable adversaries. But COPIRG also has to cope with another source of trouble: the repeated attempts to dismantle it on the part of some regents, College Republicans, and self-proclaimed right-wing students.

At the University of Colorado campus in Boulder, the administration unilaterally removed the negative check-off for all groups, including COPIRG and forty-five other organizations. The change was to begin in the spring of 1983. Since students had voted in 1976 and 1979 specifically for a negative check-off for COPIRG, the group did not accept the administration's offer of a positive check-off. Instead, the COPIRG chapter held a referendum for approval of a mandatory refundable fee. In the largest fall voter turnout on the campus since 1967, students voted overwhelmingly—2 to 1—in favor of the COPIRG fee. But the administration would not allow COPIRG to collect the $2.50-per-semester fee students had voted for.

In contrast, the CU-Boulder athletic department found itself $1 million in debt a few years before. A losing football team had failed to draw audiences and the department had to find funding for women's sports or risk violating the federal Title IX regulation that requires funding for women's athletics to be equivalent to that for men's programs. A referendum was held to increase student fees $20 per year to support the ailing program. Students voted 2 to 1 *against* the fee. The regents instituted the fee anyway. The fee has been collected every year since, without giving students another vote on the issue.

After the COPIRG referendum, the CU student government voted to fund the PIRG. The first method it approved, a mandatory refundable fee, was overturned by the president's office; the second method, a mandatory fee, was sent by the president to certain death before the regents. Under the proposal, all line items in the student government budget, including COPIRG, would have been mandatory. COPIRG, while preferring a mandatory but refundable fee, agreed to the new structure, since it would have eliminated regents' oversight. However, the regents' decision to reject the proposal left them with a line-item veto over the entire student government budget. The regents overruled the student government decision to fund the PIRG.

It was the first time in years the regents rejected a student government funding decision. The regents said they denied funding for COPIRG because they philosophically disagreed with the idea of a student-supported mandatory fee, regardless of whether it was refundable. NYPIRG's Tom Wathen, who is a former executive director of COPIRG, says, "It should be left up to the students to decide if they agree with the philosophy behind a student fee." The rejections of the students' decisions show that "there's not much appreciation for democracy" by regents at the Boulder campus, according to Wathen.

Tim Lange, editor of the *Colorado Daily* in Boulder, said the newspaper received a large outpouring of mail opposing the regents' decision not to fund the PIRG. Students were angry that COPIRG took all the appropriate steps and then was thwarted by the regents, Lange said. The Board of Regents have also instituted other restrictions on students' rights: It revamped the student discipline code so that the university can punish students, with suspension or expulsion, for off-campus behavior, and according to Lange, the regents threatened to cut funding for the usually independent Cultural Events Board when it planned to sponsor controversial speakers as part of a program on Central America.

Wathen says the limitations on students' rights being imposed by the regents is one of the biggest problems students face. But the regents are not the only problem. The students' right to fund an organization or project is coming under attack by another group, the College Republicans.

While CU was struggling to regain funding, some

members of the College Republicans at CSU–Fort Collins petitioned to hold a referendum on COPIRG's funding system. COPIRG lost the referendum, but then it was discovered that those students opposing the PIRG had misrepresented the nature of the COPIRG fee when they asked for signatures on petitions. Most of the petitions were thrown out, and the referendum was declared invalid. The next year, 1982–83, COPIRG placed itself on a ballot so students could vote legitimately about the PIRG's funding. Students approved the COPIRG refusable-refundable fee in that election.

While individual COPIRG chapters were fighting such reactionary opposition on campus, they also had to fight for survival in the state capitol.

Representative Frank DeFilippo, Republican of Golden, sponsored a bill to eliminate COPIRG's funding by prohibiting the use of student fees for "activity of a political nature without prior approval." Not only would the bill have eliminated COPIRG's fee, it would have prevented such things as student government elections or sponsorship of political speakers—from the president of the United States on down to city council members—by student government or other groups funded by student fees. DeFilippo's proposal ignores the "prior approval" students give for a COPIRG fee when they vote in referendums.

An editorial in the *Rocky Mountain News*, a Denver-based newspaper, stated: "Incredible as it may seem, Colorado's representatives of democratic government have taken aim at students' learning the process of democratic government. Could be that the young people in Colorado colleges have simply learned how to participate in the political process too well."

The editorial went on to say the bill ". . . is a slap at students who think that part of higher education involves learning how the democratic system works and who, through student-controlled COPIRGs, have learned to affect issues and problems they care about."

Carl Miller of the *Denver Post* wrote, "As so often happens at the state Capitol, a whole bunch of worthwhile things have been put in jeopardy just because a few politicians in the legislature want to get rid of a pet peeve."

Both papers urged legislators to "give this proposal the trouncing it deserves." They were joined by students, COPIRG, and university administrators. The regents also opposed the bill because it would have taken away their authority to supervise the use of student fees.

Moorman, then chairperson of the state board at CSU, recalls the close fight to defeat the bill. When it was first introduced, it was "shoved through committee" without advance notice. The College Republicans were at the hearing, testifying in favor of the bill. Moorman says she and other PIRG members built a coalition of student groups, testified before the legislature, and explained the issue to editorial boards of newspapers. Still, she says she "was never confident we would win." Consequently, Moorman had to spend all of her time on the DeFilippo bill, abandoning plans to promote higher-education issues such as guaranteeing student grants, minority loans, and scholarships to broaden access to colleges.

Despite the victory for PIRG in 1983, no one in COPIRG thinks they have seen the last of the attacks. "As long as we are promoting issues that affect powerful special interests, we will have opposition," says Megan Seibel, COPIRG's executive director. And Curt Stringer, who was state board chairperson of COPIRG in 1983–84, says, "When special interest groups attack us it shows we're effective."

"It remains to be seen what will happen when we start to be stronger, with more community involvement," Seibel says. Either way, she believes that with increasing support in the community and on campus, COPIRG will be able to weather the attacks and come out even stronger.

## MAKING IT HAPPEN

A look at COPIRG's successful work proves what can be done, despite the time spent deflecting attacks:

- Voter Registration—COPIRG's Motor Voter Initiative passed, enabling citizens to register when getting or renewing their driver's licenses.
- Higher Education Funding—a research and education project to inform the public about federal cutbacks in financial aid. COPIRG generated thousands of letters from citizens to members of Congress asking them to maintain funding for higher education.
- Poudre River Preservation—Students testified against the construction of dams along the Poudre canyon. COPIRG argued environmental damages would be significant and that the plan would be economically unsound. Plans for the dams have been scrapped, and now COPIRG is supporting preservation of the river under the Wild and Scenic Rivers Act, which would allow continued popular activity on the river such as fishing, kayaking, and swimming.
- Clean Air Act—COPIRG conducted a statewide petition drive to preserve the federal Clean Air Act. More than twelve thousand signatures were gathered by students and forwarded to Colorado's United States senators, Gary Hart and William Armstrong.
- Consumer Complaint Hotline—Students staffed a telephone complaint service to give free, non-legal counseling on consumer problems.

COPIRG also held educational forums with academic, business, governmental, and citizen experts on topics such as energy policy, health care, environmental protection, and occupational health hazards. COPIRG's candidate forums with local and state candidates of both parties also attracted a broad cross-section of the public.

COPIRG has produced guides on topics such as auto insurance, as well as "How to Complain About Anything," a handbook on consumer rights and resources. COPIRG's major publication, however, is its quarterly newsletter, *Colorado Outlook*.

The newsletter does more than describe the problems facing Coloradans; it gives the reader information about how to combat them. The *Outlook* tells readers what COPIRG is working on, and it tells them what they can do as citizens. It gives step-by-step explanations of how a bill is passed in the legislature and advises citizens where to write on pending legislation, or how to get involved in the local decision-making processes. *Outlook* is distributed free to about twenty thousand students, and, with COPIRG's door-to-door canvass, people in the community can subscribe to it.

After the first summer of canvassing, with seventy-five people knocking on doors each day, COPIRG gained nine thousand citizen members in the community and $170,000 in contributions. Not only has the canvass allowed COPIRG to inform the community about its work and involve people in such activities as letter-writing to elected officials or local newspapers, the canvass gives the PIRG a stronger funding base.

In retrospect, the struggles COPIRG has gone through, including its low point in 1976 and almost being dismantled in 1981, provided the staff and students with lessons "that have gone into making PIRGs strong," Wathen says. Students wishing to be effective in a citizens group now see how success depends on strong funding and cohesiveness among the chapters. "Just setting up a PIRG is not enough," Wathen says.

The regents have also learned a lesson, from the 1960s, about how to defuse student protest, according to Lange. But he does not think COPIRG will fall: "They [COPIRG members] certainly have the ideas, and if they can manage to inbue new people with the fire they have," COPIRG will remain a force to be reckoned with.

Wathen agrees. He has been with the PIRGs for a long time—from his college days at the University of Indiana, to Colorado, and now at New York PIRG where he is executive director—and he has seen the PIRG movement through good times and bad. And, with a matter-of-factness that may be as characteristic of his midwestern upbringing as of his confidence in COPIRG, Wathen says, "PIRGs were started in unusual times; we'll survive in unusual times."

# SIX

# Student Activists/ Public Citizens

### KENNETH WARD

During his freshman year in college, Kenneth Ward single-handedly lobbied an energy conservation bill before the Massachusetts legislature.

To fulfill a class assignment at Hampshire College, Ward developed a conservation incentive—tying lowered vehicle registration fees to increased fuel efficiency. The course's "final exam": to draft legislation for the proposal and lobby for its passage at the State House.

Ward passed—but his bill didn't.

Looking back on the experience, Ward, currently executive director of New Jersey PIRG, recalls the conclusion he drew from that venture in lobbying: "One student, working alone, is not going to pass legislation."

Since then, Ward has helped realize his share of public interest goals, through opportunities he has found in a varied, eleven-year career with the PIRGs. He has served as a member and two-time chair of the Massachusetts PIRG Board of Directors, a lobbyist, PIRG campus organizer and canvass director, field organizer for a national PIRG campaign, and executive director of Rhode Island

PIRG. He is, according to Susan Birmingham, director of the Fund for Public Interest Research, "one of the country's foremost experts on how to organize students," and has written a dissertation on the subject.

Ward's interest in political issues, and his inclination to act on them, dates back to his years at Nathan Bishop Junior High School in Providence, Rhode Island, where he helped organize fellow students in a protest against American involvement in the Vietnam War. In high school, he joined with students from other schools around the city to put out a city-wide newspaper, for which he served as editor, that covered the politics of the Providence public education system.

Ward entered Hampshire College in Massachusetts ready to translate his concerns about the environment and safe energy issues into action. He became involved in local protests against the Montague nuclear reactor, a power station proposed for construction nearby. He also took the course in public interest advocacy taught by then Massachusetts PIRG Executive Director Jon Souwaine, the course during which Ward had lobbied the Massachusetts State House.

Ward began to change his views on how best to work for the public interest. Lobbying for his energy conservation bill taught Ward that outside pressure from citizens was just as necessary for a successful legislative campaign as an insider's knowledge of capitol politics. The protests against Montague also left him feeling that, with an issue as complex as that of nuclear power, "a research approach would be more effective than just straight demonstrations."

As a result of his newly developed understanding, Ward joined MASSPIRG, where he expected he could create an effective mix of well-researched proposals with well-organized campaigns for implementation. Ward began as an intern in the summer of his freshman year, investigating ways to control motor vehicle air pollution, and by his junior year, in 1978, he was chairperson of the MASSPIRG board.

MASSPIRG, before Ward became involved, was "almost exclusively a campus-based, research-oriented organization," he recalls. Before becoming board chair, he started laying the groundwork for shifting the group's focus so that it became a more sophisticated, "campaign-type" organization.

As part of this new focus, MASSPIRG, in the spring of 1980, initiated its Citizen Outreach Project, a door-to-door citizen education and fundraising project, which has enlisted more than 105,000 Massachusetts residents as citizen PIRG members. The project has served as a model for PIRG canvasses in other states.

MASSPIRG also took the lead in fostering a national PIRG movement with the launching of the Campaign for Safe Energy (CSE). CSE was designed to make the issues of nuclear reactor safety and alternative energy development central to the 1980 presidential election campaign.

The Democratic convention, in response to CSE, adopted a party platform plank calling for the eventual closing of all nuclear power plants and for a major federal commitment to conservation and alternative energy. Ward and his colleagues subsequently built up sufficient delegate pressure on Carter forces at the convention to obtain a prime-time slot for a nationally televised safe-energy speech by Congressman Edward Markey from Massachusetts.

Having helped promote a national PIRG issue with CSE, Ward himself went on to become a leading figure in the PIRG movement. In 1980, after serving his second term as board chair, Ward took the organizing and legislative skills he had learned back to his native state to serve as executive director of Rhode Island PIRG (RIPIRG). In

Rhode Island, he oversaw a successful organizing and funding drive at the University of Rhode Island. While leading RIPIRG's initial campaigns for a state bottle bill and for a consumers' utility board, Ward initiated such consumer projects as a tenant hotline and an auto repair survey.

After two years at RIPIRG, Ward went to work for the California PIRG in the fall of 1982. In addition to working on CALPIRG's bottle bill campaign, Ward served as a campus organizer at UCLA, CALPIRG's largest chapter. At UCLA he successfully negotiated a PIRG fee system and further developed the approaches that have made him a leading expert on student organizing.

The experience Ward gained as a canvass director, organizer, and executive director provided him with the vital skills needed and utilized for his next and current position—executive director of New Jersey PIRG. When Ward took over that job in the spring of 1983, the organization faced major funding problems. A large number of staff funded through Volunteers in Service to America (VISTA) grants had been lost when those grants were terminated by the Reagan administration in 1981.

In addition, the NJPIRG fee collection method used at Rutgers University had been under attack since 1979, when a group of students, backed by the conservative Mid-Atlantic Legal Foundation, sought to have the PIRG fee declared unconstitutional. A lower court decision in NJPIRG's favor was overturned by an appeals court, and the U.S. Supreme Court declined to hear the case, leaving the appeals court decision standing.

As a result of that decision, efforts were undertaken at Rutgers to establish a different fee system. With the support of over 85 percent of the students voting in referenda, of university faculty and alumni, and of the state's top political leaders, NJPIRG and Rutgers University agreed in 1986 to adopt a waivable fee system akin to those used at other public colleges across the nation.

To bolster citizen support for NJPIRG and to broaden its funding base, NJPIRG initiated a citizen outreach based on the citizen canvass Ward had helped design for MASSPIRG. The NJPIRG canvass has enlisted more than thirty-five thousand members.

While keeping NJPIRG on a firm footing, Ward found the time to supervise campaigns establishing impressive legislative and legal victories. For example, the group helped pass a toxics right-to-know law giving chemical workers and neighboring towns the right to information on chemicals produced, handled, and stored by New Jersey companies. By the summer of 1986, NJPIRG had won fifteen initial court victories in "clean water" lawsuits against New Jersey firms accused of illegal water pollution. And, after other groups had failed for thirteen years, NJPIRG persuaded the state Assembly to hold its first-ever floor vote on a New Jersey bottle bill.

Ward sees a "bright future" for the public interest in New Jersey. The description could as well apply to his PIRG career. The relatively young executive director has gained a breadth of experience unusual even among the PIRGs. Kenneth Ward has shown how much one can learn from working with the organizations and, with such knowledge, how fast and how far one can go in promoting social change.

## JILL SIEGEL

Jill Siegel was the kind of student Ralph Nader could point to and say, "I told you so." "I told you students had the creativity and drive needed to bring about social change." "I told you, 'Once a public citizen, always a public citizen.'"

The story of her involvement with the New York Public Interest Research Group, and the public interest work she has continued since college, is a textbook example of the case Nader was trying to make when he was promoting the idea of students as "ideal activists."

Siegel grew up in Queens (one of the boroughs that make up New York City), and went to Bryant High School there. She was a cheerleader, on the tennis team, social secretary of the senior class (which meant she organized dances, fundraisers, and other class activities), and she was a member of the future-teachers club. She wanted to be a math teacher one day. It was in the early seventies, and the ecology movement was growing. Siegel added a high-school ecology club to the list of her activities.

In her first year at the State University of New York at Buffalo, Siegal's interest in environmental issues led her to join the New York Public Interest Research Group. She worked with other students to educate the campus about recycling garbage. She was primarily interested in ecology issues, but she got involved in other projects as well. She was used to taking on activities outside of classes.

One project, she recalls, entailed gathering information about the state's legislators—how their constituents viewed them, their accessibility, their stands on the issues. The profile project was a mammoth undertaking for NYPIRG because the group was still young and the profiles were to be not just a compilation of voting records, but a comprehensive view of the Assembly and Senate members. Students such as Siegel volunteered to scour local papers, talk to political leaders, community groups, and constituents, and study how the legislators voted. Siegel remembers that was her first exposure to the workings of state government.

From that introduction to the legislative process, Siegel decided to participate in NYPIRG's Legislative Internship Program during her sophomore year. By the end of the semester-long internship, the nineteen-year-old, who had been studying environmental design and was still toying with the idea of teaching, had lobbied a bill into law. Her plans would never be quite the same.

Siegel was the first student to participate full time in the legislative program, in the spring of 1975. She had decided during the previous fall to take the internship, for which she would receive sixteen hours' credit through the political science and urban studies departments. In November, Donald Ross, who was executive director of NYPIRG and had been developing the lobbying program, suggested some bills she could work on. One was to reform hearing aid sales practices. To Siegel, still primarily interested in environmental issues, it did not seem like the most exciting legislation at first. But the need for the bill was evident. A 1974 Queens College NYPIRG study, entitled *Hear Ye, Hear Ye!*, found widespread fraud in hearing aid sales practices. The study concluded that 40 percent of the people who were sold hearing aids either did not need them at all or actually had serious medical problems that needed a doctor's attention. Yet hearing aid dealers were able to fit unwary customers with the devices. Many who needed medical attention for a hearing problem were led to believe the hearing aid was sufficient; some jeopardized their hearing and their health by not seeking that medical care. Those who did not need a hearing aid at all were out considerable expense—each aid cost $300 or more.

NYPIRG developed a bill that would combat the fraud by requiring that a doctor examine the patient and prescribe a hearing aid before one could be purchased. Previously, manufacturers, distributors, and dealers had been able to sell a hearing aid to anyone requesting it. Since many aids were sold unnecessarily, the requirement of a doctor's prescription helped consumers avoid the cost of an aid they did not need. The bill also required a thirty-day money-back guarantee. In November, Siegel decided to take on the hearing aid project, and after finals, she spent her winter break studying the issue and also reading about the workings of the state capitol.

While she was able to learn a lot about hearing aid sales abuse during that time, her reading did not really prepare her for the ins and outs of lobbying. Siegel remembers approaching legislators to get a sponsor for the bill. "At that point they weren't used to student lobbyists," she says. "I didn't look very old, either," she adds. Some were still wary of NYPIRG because they did not like the sometimes unflattering revelations of the legislative profiles. It was not the best climate for the nascent NYPIRG lobbying program. So, without a high-powered reputation to wield, Siegel knew she would have to build a strong network of support for NYPIRG's bill throughout the state.

Fraud in hearing aid sales had the greatest impact on the elderly. Not only are they the most likely group to need the devices, but their usually limited incomes make it more difficult for them to absorb the cost. As the Queens College study showed, many of the purchasers did not even need hearing aids. With that in mind, Siegel spoke before senior-citizen groups such as the Gray Panthers and gained their support. She also got support from groups representing the hearing impaired and parents of hearing-impaired children, and from doctors and audiologists. Initially, they were skeptical that a student lobbyist could be effective, but once she spoke at their meetings, they were convinced she knew what was happening on the political front, and that she was well prepared to work for hearing aid sales reform. With those groups behind the bill, NYPIRG's voice in the capitol was much stronger.

During the semester, Siegel became the expert on hearing aid reform in the state. She learned her way around the capitol halls and committee rooms, and she met with legislators and their staff to promote the bill. She became so adept at lobbying that one senator's staff counsel asked Donald Ross whether NYPIRG had hired a new attorney. An incident one day proved to her that she had "gotten the hang of lobbying." She caught sight of a senator who had opposed the hearing aid bill and had refused to meet with her about it. He was walking into the men's room, so she stood outside the door until he came out, and then she cornered him. He gave in and listened to her explain the measure on the way back to his office, and he even spent an additional half hour discussing it with her. In the end, convinced by her presentation of the facts, and no doubt impressed by her persistence, the senator endorsed the bill. "From being a nervous and up-tight sophomore, I became more aggressive and poised as I went along," Siegel says. Assemblyman William Passannante, Speaker pro tem, says, "All the legislators I came in contact with thought very highly of Jill."

Her political savvy developed as well, and she learned how to give the bill the boosts it needed when it got buried in committee: "Once when our bill got stalled, we held a press conference with the sponsors. We put together a good campaign—lots of letters and telegrams—from hundreds of people. On such a relatively obscure issue, that much support is unexpected. It makes people pay a lot of attention," Siegel explained.

The support was particularly unexpected by hearing aid manufacturers. Siegel said that although the manufacturers opposed the bill, at first they didn't see her work on it as posing a threat. But when it passed through the committees, they got to work fighting it. Ross had told her from the beginning to expect a fierce battle, but Siegel admits she was a bit naive—"I knew it was a good bill and would protect the hearing impaired," she says. Legislators would not have any reason to oppose such an "apple pie" issue, or so she thought. She had to realize on her own that industry lobbyists were not looking at it from a consumer protection standpoint, and therefore would make an all-out effort to defeat it. It was not long in coming. One of the manufacturers' biggest arguments was that they serve rural communities where doctors are not readily available, and that the bill would prevent rural residents from getting any kind of help for hearing problems. Siegel "took care of that argument" by looking up all the hearing aid dealers in the state and marking their locations on the map. She found that virtually all of them were located in the same areas as doctors. When the lobbyists for the industry would send memos to legislators making such claims about the bill, Siegel would rebut them with memos of her own. Through the semester, she also helped keep the public informed about the issue by doing radio and television talk shows and panel discussions, as well as press conferences. "That gave me a lot of confidence," she says. But the ultimate vote of confidence came when the bill, after causing a rare final-day debate on the floor, was passed and signed into law by Governor Hugh Carey.

Siegel was at home in Queens at the time, since the legislative session had gone into the summer. She monitored the bill daily and made calls to members of the coalition she had developed. At that point, it was the consistent pressure from these groups that would have the most impact. Yet Siegel did not even know whether the bill would get voted on, even though it was scheduled for a debate in the Senate. "I knew it was the last day of the session, and that there was talk that it would be debated, but I couldn't be sure," she says. Ross called her from Albany that night with the good news.

Jill's father, Mike Siegel, recalls that the final day of the session was very exciting around the Siegel home. The then secretary of state, Mario Cuomo, and Assemblyman Passannante, who sponsored the bill, called Jill at home several times that day to advise her of attempts to defeat the measure. Jill then called supporters, urging them to put more pressure on legislators. The family had kept track of the bill's progress along with Jill, so it was very exciting when it did pass, the elder Siegel says. "We still have the pen [used by the governor to sign the bill] and a copy of the proclamation at home," he adds. Mr. Siegel says he was apprehensive at first when he learned Jill would be lobbying, because he did not know what it entailed. But he and Jill's mother and sister "were all involved in following Jill's exploits with NYPIRG," he says. According to Mr. Siegel, he learned a lot himself about how a bill becomes law because of Jill's work. He is also very supportive of NYPIRG—"a marvelous organization"—and besides keeping track of its projects in the newspaper, he often visits with NYPIRG "kids" when they come to his clothing store in Greenwich Village.

After the hearing aid bill passed, the Senate Consumer Protection Committee held hearings to discuss the bill's implementation. When Jill Siegel testified, some hearing aid manufacturers booed. "I knew then that I had been effective," she laughs. "My name was pretty well known at that point among the hearing aid manufacturers." It was also well known among people working on similiar reform in other states, who called Siegel about her efforts in New York. In addition, the Federal Trade Commission sought her comments when it was considering federal reform of hearing aid sales practices.

Besides learning a great deal about hearing aid reform, Siegel obviously learned a lot about the legislative process. She was the first full-time legislative intern for NYPIRG (others worked part-time that semester) so she was called on to speak to potential interns about the program. She pointed out to students that as a NYPIRG intern she got a much wider perspective of the state government than she would have as an intern with one Assembly or Senate member—which was how the university set up internships. As an advocate, she talked with many legislators and staff members, became familiar with a number of committees, and, of course, saw first hand how a bill becomes law. Siegel reported, too, that no classroom lecture could compare with the learning that takes place when you have to convince a legislator that a bill deserves his or her vote, or when you have to rally support for a bill in the community. "Being there first hand was what really taught me about the legislature," Siegel says. She also learned what one does *not* need to know to be a lobbyist: "You don't have to have tons of knowledge to become an effective lobbyist," she said. Selected, solid facts in a particular area, clearly presented, can do the trick. "You learn not to be intimidated by issues" because you can grasp them if you are willing to take the time, she adds.

During the next two years of college, she served as chairperson of the SUNY Buffalo PIRG's local board of directors, taught a class on public interest research in the urban studies program with two other PIRG members, worked on voter registration on campus, wrote a guide to medical services for women in Buffalo, and coordinated press conferences. She also spent time "lobbying" on campus to get support for NYPIRG. Although she wanted to, she did not spend another semester in Albany—staying on would not have earned further course credits, which she needed, and "I don't think they would have given me a degree in lobbying," she jokes.

The degree she did get was in political science—changed from environmental design after the internship. During her senior year, she decided to go to law school. The work of the lawyers on the NYPIRG staff, including Ross and Nancy Kramer, led Siegel to realize that legal training would be a useful tool for a citizen activist. Assemblyman Passannante says he used to tease Siegel, asking her, "Why do you want to get into government and starve like me? You should go work for a big law firm and make lots of money." Siegel would have none of it, and of course, Passannante was not surprised.

She chose Antioch School of Law in Washington, D.C. Antioch has an extensive clinical program, which allows its students to get hands-on experience in a variety of areas of law, and the school places emphasis on providing legal help to those in need. Siegel liked that emphasis on learning-by-doing, since she had become familiar with it through NYPIRG. "I always have felt that through college most of my true learning was gleaned from working with NYPIRG," she said. At Antioch, she worked in such areas as prisoners' rights, consumer and administrative law, and tenants' rights. She was also an intern on Senator Edward Kennedy's Judiciary Committee, and she served as a law clerk for the Federal Trade Commission's consumer protection bureau. She would not have been qualified for that position if she had not been a NYPIRG student lobbyist and become familiar with consumer issues through NYPIRG, she says.

After law school, she returned to New York to work as—what else?—a lobbyist for the Bronx Legal Services, promoting reform in family and housing law, as well as in Social Security programs. Now, as its staff attorney, Siegel handles family law cases of custody and child abuse and neglect, landlord-tenant cases, and cases where people have been refused welfare or Medicaid services.

Siegel remembers that after the hearing aid bill passed in 1975, Donald Ross said to her, "I guess in certain ways you'll never be the same person." Recalling his words years later, Siegel lists the things she never would have done if not for having the experience with NYPIRG: work as an advocate for a New York group on reform of funeral restrictions, attend law school at Antioch in Washington, D.C., work for the Federal Trade Commission's consumer protection bureau, or hold her current position with Bronx Legal Services in New York. All of those pursuits, she says, came about because of qualifications and interests that she developed through the internship and through other projects she did for NYPIRG.

As a cheerleader in Bryant High School, or even as a first-year college student promoting ecology issues, Jill Siegel would not likely have guessed she would be an attorney now, a dozen years later. Even now, Siegel does not pretend to know where she will be in another dozen years. But she says, without hesitation, it will involve the kind of public interest work that she didn't even really know existed before she walked into a NYPIRG office.

## BOB CHLOPAK

Siegel's story is not uncommon. Many students start college not knowing what they want to do for the next four years—much less for the rest of their lives. They have some idea what college is about: all-night cramming for tests, dorm food, living away from home, parties, and probably a part-time job. Since it is unlikely they were exposed to citizen activism in high school, they often do not see it as part of their college years either. And often, having heard about only the noisiest manifestations of campus unrest—student demonstrations, rallies, and violent reprisals—they do not come to college thinking in terms of being an activist through a staffed organization such as a public interest research group.

Bob Chlopak, then, is an exception. From his first day as a student at George Washington University in Washington, D.C., Chlopak was searching for an outlet for his political interests and social concerns. He had joined the now defunct Student Mobilization Committee, an antiwar group, but he found its vitality to be waning, just as the war was. Chlopak had been involved in some antiwar protests in high school, albeit the subdued protests one would expect from a Dumont, New Jersey, high school. By

1972 when he began college, he says, "I felt the antiwar movement was phasing out; I wanted to be part of something that would build and grow." Student government was not the answer. For one thing, the student government at GWU had voted to abolish itself. Although it could be reestablished, Chlopak knew it was structured to address campus issues only. Chlopak was looking to get involved in the political fray beyond the protests, and beyond the campus, in a way that would do more than point out problems—he wanted to change things.

His search ended when he heard Donald Ross talk about something called a public interest research group.

"His speech made such logical sense, and the PIRG idea fit my ideas about getting involved on important issues," Chlopak says. A group of half a dozen other students started a PIRG organizing committee to set up PIRGs at the D.C. campuses of American University, Georgetown, and, of course, GWU.

"We were well intentioned and enthusiastic, but inexperienced," Chlopak remembers. All of them were in their first year of college, except one student who was a sophomore. That made them different from the PIRG organizers on other campuses then who were usually juniors, seniors, or even graduate school students.

Chlopak spent twenty-five to thirty hours or more a week petitioning, recruiting volunteers, and talking to faculty and administrators. Since GWU is an urban, commuter campus, reaching students to tell them about PIRG was difficult, but the effort turned out to be the most successful petition drive ever at GWU, with forty-seven hundred signatures. Even with that support, they were unable to get the administration to approve any funding system other than a positive check-off on registration forms, which is considerably weaker than the mandatory yet refundable fee. Chlopak still remembers the excitement of getting funding approval. "It was disappointing that we didn't get a stronger funding mechanism, but it was still thrilling that the PIRG finally became a reality."

GWU's new PIRG chose rent control as the topic for its first project, a logical choice since the staff that students had chosen was strong on housing issues and the PIRG was in an urban environment. Also, during that time, with inflation driving the price of everything upward, people were less able to absorb stiff rent increases. Chlopak "went where the momentum carried him" and worked on a door-to-door, statistically valid survey to obtain information on rent increases, tenant security, and the ability of D.C.'s tenants to exercise their rights. The PIRG also operated a hotline to take tenant complaints, so they had a good understanding of the extent of problems faced by renters.

Soaring energy prices were the primary cause of the burgeoning cost of maintaining rental property, yet the landlords passed on all the costs and sustained their generally healthy profit margin. "The landlords weren't sharing the burden," Chlopak says. Chlopak and other researchers studied the way rent is assessed, and how much of the cost was based on energy costs. From there they developed a rent control plan. The rent control measure they proposed provided for equitable return for the landlords, while guaranteeing an affordable roof over the heads of renters.

The PIRG then presented the proposal to Congress and the D.C. City Council, organized hearings, and formed a city-wide housing coalition. "We started from scratch and succeeded in a year and a half in advocating the first rent control legislation in the District since World War Two," Chlopak notes; with that, D.C. became one of the first major cities involved in the tenant rights movement. Chlopak estimates the DCPIRG work saved millions of dollars in averted rent increases to District residents.

He said he practically lived at the city council offices, working there to get support, initially for rent control, and then for a strong enforcement commission to make sure landlords were complying with the measure. Though he did not know much about tenant/landlord issues or even how the District government was run when he went in, Chlopak says, "I stumbled my way around, asked a lot of questions. That was part of the thrill, realizing you *could* do it." In the classroom, students read about theories behind government and how it affects the people, he says, but in PIRG work, "you get to go to city hall and see the real meaning of the information you get in class, and how you could use it to affect public policy."

All of this transpired before Chlopak was twenty-one years old.

While he had been working on the rent control project, he also served on the local board of DCPIRG, where he developed administrative skills and helped shape the focus of DCPIRG projects. His original concern about having an impact outside the campus had been answered with the PIRG's work on rent control. But no one in the group, including Chlopak, wanted to stop there, so DCPIRG moved into energy issues.

By then, it was Chlopak's senior year. He led volunteers in investigating the local utility company, PEPCO, and its rate structures, rate increase proposals, and the role consumers had in the decision-making process, which led to a study of the Public Utilities Commission. DCPIRG found a need for reform. Working with a community-based group called D.C. Power, the PIRG documented the problems—lack of citizen access to the rate-setting process, rate structures that penalize the low-volume user, unfair shutoff practices—and proposed solutions. Their success can be marked by PEPCO's changed rate structure, which gives customers a lower rate per kilowatt hour for using less energy; PEPCO's holding hearings on rate increases so people in the community can testify without being an official party to the required hearings before the PUC, and the utility's new policy giving longer notice before shutting off electricity.

DCPIRG also discovered a study, done by a consultant for investor-owned utilities, on utility-company efficiency. It rated PEPCO twenty-third out of twenty-four companies. That information came out just as PEPCO was asking for a large rate increase, and the PUC held special proceedings to look into the company's efficiency. PEPCO, respecting the impact a disgruntled PIRG could have, took time to meet with PIRG and D.C. Power staff to defend its record.

Lenore Pomerance, then coordinator of D.C. Power, says of Chlopak, "There weren't too many students who would extend themselves like he did." She remembers he was "quick and competent" in writing testimony and researching utility issues, and "he's a terrific worker, always upbeat about his work." She was so impressed with Chlopak that she later recommended him for a job with the organization her husband worked for—Friends of the Earth—which Chlopak accepted.

During his four years in college, Chlopak himself had gained recognition on campus because of numerous school newspaper articles about PIRG. The GWU administrators knew him well, and he was on a first name basis with the university's president. They did not always agree on the issues, Chlopak says, but they respected each other. William P. Smith, vice president for student affairs, notes that working for PIRG was "very much of an educational experience for those involved." Smith says sometimes "there was a conflict of views [particularly on how to fund the PIRG], but despite that we got along very well."

In between all the involvement with PIRG, Chlopak had time to get a degree in political science. Then, at age twenty-three, he was going to leave it all behind. Graduation. Maybe law school. The days with PIRG were over, a college-years' activity, right? Hardly.

Chlopak did leave PIRG for a few months to travel around and consider what he wanted to do with his life. He had always planned to work for a member of Congress, thinking that would be a way to be at the center of political reform. But being involved with PIRG took the luster off congressional work because "it [working in Congress] doesn't give you a chance to really make a difference." The kind of reform-oriented work he did with PIRG figured largely in his plan. When he arrived back in D.C., he found out he figured largely in DCPIRG's plans, too. The PIRG hired him as research director. With Randy Swisher, also one of the first organizers of DCPIRG, he arranged to teach a two-semester course at Georgetown University: Energy, Utilities, and the Public Interest, one section of a loosely structured sociology course. "It was really fruitful; it allowed us to take PIRG into the classroom. We had students work on the PEPCO project, researching the economic aspects of nuclear power. I think the students were really positive about it too." They must have been, because Chlopak and Swisher were asked to repeat the course the following year.

In the summer of 1977, at a conference of PIRGs from across the United States, the state PIRGs voted to set up a new organization, National PIRG, to be a clearinghouse and to help coordinate organizing efforts and other projects in which PIRGs in several states could participate. The National PIRG was to be funded with small contributions from each PIRG. When they set up the national office in D.C., they asked Chlopak to come on staff. "I was called and asked where my resume was—I didn't take it seriously—then they called and asked if I wanted the job," Chlopak says. Since he had been with DCPIRG for six years, he decided to make the change. One of National PIRG's first projects was to administer a Volunteers in

Service to America (VISTA) grant. The grant was used to place VISTA volunteers in community service jobs with PIRGs throughout the country. State PIRGs designed projects for VISTA volunteers, and the National PIRG trained and placed them. Most volunteers were people with college degrees who were interested in citizen action but had little experience. Chlopak helped get them involved in projects ranging from organizing tenants and neighborhoods to setting up food purchasing co-ops.

At the next year's PIRG conference, Chlopak was named executive director of National PIRG. The group went on to develop materials for PIRG-sponsored nuclear power teach-ins, and it helped organize the successful May 6, 1979, antinuclear rally in Washington, D.C. It was the largest outdoor citizen rally since the protests of the 1960s. With the problems that caused the accident at Three Mile Island still unresolved, thousands of people gathered at the Lincoln Memorial to hear people such as Barry Commoner and Ralph Nader speak out against the danger and high cost of nuclear power.

National PIRG also played a role in PIRGs' work on reforming the Educational Testing Service (ETS). National PIRG helped line up qualified witnesses to testify in the states where PIRGs were working on the issue, and it received a grant to do teach-ins on "truth-in-testing."

Eventually, though, with many PIRGs having to focus on budget concerns for their own campus and community work, the contributions for National PIRG dwindled. In late 1979, the national office closed. (U.S. PIRG—another collective PIRG effort—was started in 1984.)

When he accepted his next job, Chlopak might have asked himself if he was destined to work with PIRGs for life. It was with MASSPIRG's Campaign for Safe Energy, which, as noted, sought to raise energy issues during the 1980 presidential campaign. After developing a platform advocating a moratorium on nuclear power plant construction and stepped-up research into solar and other renewable energy sources, the CSE needed organizers to take the campaign to the public and to the delegates at party platform conventions.

While students in MASSPIRG traveled to political rallies in the New England states and persistently questioned candidates about their stand on energy issues, Chlopak was working behind the scenes to secure support from the delegates to the platform conventions, whose votes could determine what planks each party adopted for its platform. He also lined up witnesses to testify in favor of the goals of CSE at regional platform committee hearings.

With the nuclear-power advocate Ronald Reagan certain to win the Republican party nomination, the CSE turned all its attention to the Democratic party. Chlopak found considerable support for the goals of the CSE among the delegates, spurred by the national media attention the CSE was generating and by students and staff calling delegates to promote the campaign. In the end, the party adopted virtually all of CSE's wording in its platform, over the objection of President Jimmy Carter, the party's nominee.

Next, Chlopak applied the organizing skills he had been learning to a political campaign in New York. Mark Green, a former Nader Raider and author of *Who Runs Congress?*, was running for Congress himself. He was running against a man named Bill Green. Chlopak supervised polling and found supporters in three hundred to four hundred apartment buildings who signed on to distribute information about candidate *Mark* Green; he also headed up a "get out the vote" effort on election day. But Bill Green won the election.

Disappointments, compared with his impressive early victories? Maybe, but you could not get Chlopak to describe it that way. As for the Campaign for Safe Energy,

Chlopak had seen it receive the attention of presidential candidates and endorsement from some of them. It also received national media attention, as did MASSPIRG for its efforts, so the goal of bringing energy issues to the forefront was reached. Everyone involved in the campaign learned a great deal about the political process and how to be a part of it, and people in the communities also got a sense of how citizen power can force candidates to address important community concerns. And Chlopak also learned a great deal more about organizing just by working on Mark Green's campaign. Winning isn't everything, Chlopak will tell you.

At age thirty-two, surrounded by political activists, Chlopak still does not know many his own age who have been doing political organizing for as long as he has—since age eighteen when he organized DCPIRG. Perhaps the greatest single value of a PIRG, Chlopak says, is that it produces a new crop, year after year, of trained activists. "They have the capacity to act, they learn the ropes working with professionals in a number of different situations, and they really shine under pressure.

"I owe everything that I am and have become and may do to shaping from PIRG," Chlopak says matter-of-factly. Then: "Does that sound corny? Corny or not, it's a fact."

## MARJY FISHER

Marjy Fisher met once with Martin Luther King, Jr., in Atlanta, Georgia. Yet, if you ask her why she got involved with public interest work, beginning with the Indiana PIRG, she does not mention the meeting with King as you might expect—probably because she was only three years old at the time. When reminded of the meeting, all Marjy recalls is spilling a soft drink on King's lap. It is her mother who mentions the time she took Marjy along to the forty-five-minute interview King gave to Marjy's older brother for a class project. Helen Fisher makes note of the meeting to explain how the whole family has always had an interest in social justice issues, and to explain that it seemed natural for Marjy to work with the Indiana PIRG when she began college.

Although her mom had never heard of public interest research groups when Marjy began college, she liked the idea of Marjy getting involved from the start. "I thought it was a good beginning, and that it might lead to a job or at least part-time work on those issues," Helen Fisher says.

Marjy says now that, without a doubt, working for PIRG has led to a variety of jobs she may not have otherwise gotten, and to a lifelong commitment to public interest work.

Fisher went to the University of Indiana at the age of seventeen after completing all her Columbus, Ohio, high school requirements in just three years. She wanted to go to a big state school, with a diverse student body, and Indiana fit the bill; it had the added attractions of being relatively inexpensive and close to home. With more than thirty thousand students, mammoth lecture sessions, and Big Ten football and basketball teams, the University of Indiana was typical of the huge midwestern state schools. "It was very difficult to find challenging things to do there," Fisher recalls. She wasn't interested in the popular fraternity/sorority scene, so initially she invested most of her time in classwork. But she wanted to do more.

Fisher was living in what was called the Living Learning Center (LLC), an alternative to dorm housing that offered some of its own courses and programs. It was through the LLC that she found an outlet for her interests beyond the classroom: the Indiana Public Interest Research Group (INPIRG).

The LLC offered internships with INPIRG, and following a friend's suggestion, Fisher applied for one. She was awarded the internship, but at the time it seemed like a mixed blessing. INPIRG was barely holding on. PIRG's investigations of corporations and institutions angered the school's trustees—many of whom had a financial interest in the targets of PIRG probes. The trustees stripped INPIRG of its funding check-off and required cumbersome forms for students wishing to donate to the PIRG. With the subsequent reduction in contributions, the PIRG was forced to reduce its activity. Many of the students at Indiana University were more interested in boosting the football team than in boosting the weakened PIRG, so Fisher had her work cut out for her when she was assigned to do publicity and fundraising for INPIRG.

Though she had no experience in either area, she raised a few thousand dollars during her summer internship. She developed a program to sell "INPIRG bonds" to small business owners, and she organized faculty fundraisers to get professors and teachers involved with INPIRG. "Some of the business people were wary," Fisher says, "because INPIRG did so much in the area of market surveys." The business owners knew their service or product could be scrutinized by thorough INPIRG researchers, but they still gave the struggling PIRG a vote of confidence.

Fisher struggled herself, and, like INPIRG, she survived. "It was a really hard summer because I didn't know what I was doing at first. . . . But I tried and I learned a lot and I stuck with it through the fall."

When school started again that fall of 1976, Fisher came on staff for INPIRG, adding twenty or thirty hours a week of fundraising to her already crowded class schedule. With the students back for another semester, the focus shifted to on-campus work, and Fisher dutifully trooped off day after day: organizing door-to-door solicitations in the dorms, and giving speeches to campus groups, fraternities, sororities, and dorm governing councils. "My contribution then was 'networking,'" she says, "publicizing the PIRG. It was very important to keep that student base of support, to make students aware of what we were doing."

After that hectic semester, Fisher found that going to school full time and being on staff was too much. She left the staff, but she didn't drop out of the PIRG. In the spring 1977 semester, she worked with the local board, primarily on an extended study of product liability. Some legislators were proposing that manufacturers only be responsible for injuries caused by their product within five years after the purchase date. INPIRG believed that standard would unfairly hamper consumers' ability to sue for injuries or damages caused by unsafe products, so the group took its arguments to the state legislature. The law offered consumers nothing at all: no additional savings, no additional safety. In fact, it left them with quite the opposite: an incentive for unscrupulous manufacturers to build their products to last for only five years, at which point they would be out of the reach of the law. INPIRG managed to stop the bill that session, and they won a limited victory the next year when the liability limitation was passed but was increased to ten years.

Fisher stayed with the PIRG through her junior year at Indiana University, becoming chairperson of the local board, and continuing to push PIRG on campus. "People there aren't always responsive to public interest issues," she recalls. "It was a very social school." With all the work she was doing for INPIRG, her own social life was somewhat limited: "There were some sacrifices, but there weren't all that many. I met people. It wasn't like I put in a sixty-hour week every week. I couldn't. I think I lost a couple of points on my GPA." If points off her GPA meant she missed learning something in class, Fisher is certain she made up for it with all she learned in PIRG. "I learned a lot from it. It was an alternative to boring classroom situations."

## MORE ACTION FOR A CHANGE

After two years of PIRG work, Fisher went to Washington, D.C., in the summer of 1978 to be an intern for the Pension Rights Center. She was asked to do something she had never done before—but Fisher was used to that after working for INPIRG. The center wanted her to organize a national conference on retirement income reform. Most pension conferences, she explains, are designed to help employers; this conference was aimed at helping older people who were being cheated out of pensions and security. Throughout the summer, Fisher was immersed in the project, patching together the logistics, finding speakers (Ralph Nader and Senator Howard Metzenbaum were among them), and putting together conference materials for the more than two hundred in attendance. Karen Ferguson, of the Pension Rights program, said, "If Donald Ross could have conjured up the type of person he wanted for PIRGs it would have been Marjy. She's interested, bright, energetic, and full of ideas."

That fall, Fisher finished her degree at Indiana. It didn't take her long to find something to do after graduation; it was back to Washington and public interest work, this time as an organizer for Ralph Nader's Congress Watch.

Fisher was given two primary responsibilities: informing the public about important consumer and environmental legislation, and setting up "Congress Watch" locals. These groups monitor the votes of their Congress members and keep constituents informed about consumer issues. Fisher met with the heads of local community groups to organize coalitions and to keep track of their elected representatives. "Just making a phone call from Washington doesn't always work," she says. "It's making personal contact that really involves people."

So Fisher spent seven months traveling through Miami, New Orleans, Austin, Houston, and other cities, holding meetings and explaining issues. In one case, she helped organize a town meeting in Florida with U.S. Congressman Dan Mica. The residents were well informed about his record, and hundreds were there to question him on his voting. Fisher recalls Congressman Mica saying afterward that it was at times like those he wondered why he ran for office.

At twenty-one years old, Fisher often looked out of place in the communities she was organizing, such as the retirement villages in Florida. But she found the age difference didn't matter when it came to concern about elected officials—she would often have two or three hundred citizens turn out for meetings.

When Fisher set up a Congress Watch local and a fundraiser in her hometown of Columbus, Ohio, she had the support of her mom, who helped prepare food, gave Congress Watch organizers a place to stay, and became active in the group herself. Helen Fisher was seeing her prediction come true: "Marjy's interest in activism all started with the PIRG at Indiana." Marjy agrees. "I wasn't committed to that kind of work until I started [at IN-PIRG], then I loved it."

Fisher also had an interest in studying law. As she organized small community groups, she saw the need many of them had for someone who knew the legal ropes. After a year of setting up the Congress Watch locals, she began law school at George Washington University National Law Center in Washington, D.C.

It was far from the end of her activist days, though.

She quickly discovered that the hundreds of people studying law at GWU were not being exposed to certain aspects of the legal profession—namely public interest law. "Administrators in the law school made it seem like alternative careers were not all that interesting," Fisher says. The placement center devoted just one day a year to a public interest jobs fair, and the only organizations represented were the CIA, the FBI, and the Army. Fisher and several other students staged a protest of the organizations that were masquerading as public interest groups. Wearing trench coats and dark sunglasses, the students passed out leaflets telling students about real alternative law careers.

But Fisher knew passing out leaflets wouldn't be enough. So, after being elected president of the Student Bar Association, she invited attorneys from public interest organizations and law firms to speak at informal lunch meetings on campus. The meetings were popular, attracting hundreds of people—twice as many as attended panels on corporate law, Fisher says.

Fisher also worked with the school's Law Placement Office, informing it about the myriad of positions for attorneys concerned about social justice issues. Ginny Pierce, with the placement office, credits Fisher with "making us all focus on those career options. She was responsible for the placement center working with public interest groups, and we now sponsor speakers from those organizations." The library has also added guidebooks to legal career alternatives, Pierce notes.

In order to give students exposure to public interest law, Fisher founded the Equal Justice Foundation (EJF) at GWU. EJF, like PIRG, is funded by student contributions at law schools across the nation. Students pledge 1 percent of their law income to the organization. EJF focuses on improving access to the legal system—lobbying, litigating, publishing, and training law students are among its activities.

Pierce says that the EJF gives public interest options a high profile on campus, and "keeps us [the placement center] thinking about it." Because of that presence, it is not likely that future career fairs at GWU on social change law will feature the CIA, FBI, or Army.

During law school, Fisher also worked as a law clerk for the League of Women Voters litigation branch, and later with a law firm that handled product liability cases and race and sex discrimination suits.

She says her experience at INPIRG and with Congress Watch gave her skills and credentials that helped her get those positions. Though INPIRG was a small PIRG, Fisher said potential employers still recognized the value of her work there. "It's the idea and the philosophy of the group that people look at, not just its size," Fisher says. In addition, "when you build an organization from nothing and just keep at it, that teaches you something too."

Fisher is currently an assistant district attorney in Brooklyn. "This is a job," she says. "Working for public interest groups is a lifestyle." And it's not a lifestyle Fisher expects to leave behind.

While she is with the DA's office, she will learn courtroom technique and try to specialize in economic fraud and corporate crime. She also will keep the old ties to public interest groups. "I definitely want to be in the movement," she says. "I love the work, and the people are the most interesting around. Besides," she adds, "I've never had a public interest job I wasn't interested in."

## JIM ROKAKIS

Jim Rokakis is probably the only PIRG board member who has run for a seat on the city council of a major American city while still in college.

He is undoubtedly the only one who has been elected. Rokakis began running for the council seat in Cleveland's Ward 6 during January 1977, his senior year at Oberlin College. Four months after he finished school he won the election. At twenty-two, he was the youngest person to ever serve on the Cleveland City Council. Yet that was not even his first encounter with politics. Five years earlier—at the age of seventeen—he worked for George McGovern in the 1972 presidential election, running a neighborhood office with eight employees. Two years later, he spent an entire year working as an aide to a state legislator.

Is Rokakis something of a prodigy?

"No, not really," he says with a laugh. "In neighborhoods like mine it was really hard to find somebody [to work for good government issues]. Besides," he says, "I grew up with the sixties burning in my conscience." The Vietnam War, coupled with the Watergate revelations in the seventies of widespread corruption in government, left Rokakis with a desire to right some of the wrongs in the system. There were plenty to be concerned with in his own backyard.

Rokakis's neighborhood was the southwest side of Cleveland, a working-class ethnic neighborhood. Most residents had little formal education or money. The economic well-being of Cleveland, and in fact the entire industrial northeast, was in decline. As a result, crime, poverty, a shrinking tax base, and racial and ethnic polarization had taken an undue toll on the city. On December 15, 1978, it fell to default—becoming only the second major city (after New York, in 1976) to do so since the Depression.

The default was precipitated by a bitter struggle between the city's mayor, young Dennis Kucinich; the city council, led by George Forbes; and the city's banks, headed by Brock Weir of the Cleveland Trust Company. Rokakis, just one year out of school, was right in the middle of the action, there for the endless, almost surrealistic debates on the city council floor, and the even stormier backdoor meetings where the real decisions were made.

Rokakis became involved with PIRG during the first semester of his senior year. After attending Case Western Reserve for a year, and spending a year working for State

Senator Charles Butts in Columbus, Rokakis found the decision to join PIRG at Oberlin an easy one. "It was the only thing on campus I could relate to in any way, shape, or form," he says.

The PIRG at Oberlin—a well-regarded liberal arts school—was only a little more than a year old when Rokakis was elected to the board of directors, but he remembers, "it had a great impact on campus. It involved a lot of students. . . . There wasn't that kind of activism elsewhere. PIRG probably stirred more interest on campus than anything else."

It stirred up some changes in Rokakis as well. "I think PIRG made me much more aware," he says. "I was very skeptical about the antinuclear movement, for example. In my neighborhood, the concerns were more local things like getting a job and eating and walking to the corner without getting mugged. . . . But [the nuclear issue] was possibly more important than some of the things I was interested in because of its long-term effects."

Rokakis and other Oberlin PIRG students spent much of their time that year working against nuclear power. They focused on a plant in Port Clinton being built by Babcock/Wilcox, the same firm whose equipment was in the Three Mile Island plant that had a near melt-down. The students produced information packets on the nuclear issue and spoke throughout their area to neighborhood groups.

Besides the nuclear fight, the Oberlin PIRG published a consumer's "best buy" handbook for residents of Lorain County; a handbook explaining a new law regulating landlord/tenant agreements; and a study, with local environmental groups, of the problems with a jetport proposed for the area. The jetport was scuttled.

Being the only Ohio-born student on the board—Oberlin traditionally attracts students from a wide mix of states—"I had special responsibilities," Rokakis says, "because I had worked in Ohio politics. I became the person to see on the state legislature." By the middle of his senior year, Rokakis was no longer working on Ohio politics—he was working in them.

"Some people [at school] were very supportive and some were skeptical," Rokakis says about reactions to his candidacy. "I think people in the neighborhood were skeptical [too]," he continues, "but it was recognized by politicians across town that we ran a very aggressive campaign." In the beginning, the campaign was run primarily on weekends, squeezed in between classes, papers, and assignments. With a schedule like that, he says, "there's no such thing as a social life." But Rokakis and his supporters plugged away, picking up the hours once school let out. Eventually they knocked on each of the six thousand doors in the ward—*twice*. They published a neighborhood newsletter—which Rokakis is still publishing ten years later. Rokakis was the first city council member in Cleveland to produce such a newsletter for his constituents; now six other members have followed suit.

The way to the council seat was cleared when the incumbent decided to step aside. Running on a platform that included bread-and-butter issues such as improving municipal services and obtaining a fair share of federal community development money, as well as broader issues such as creating a housing court that would handle all housing disputes, Rokakis swept to victory in November. "I had seen my neighborhoods and my city begin to fall apart before my eyes," he says. "I felt we needed people who had a less parochial view of city government."

At that point, Cleveland needed all the help it could get.

For hours in the fall of 1978, just after taking his seat on the city council, Rokakis sat through the nightmarish debates in the council over how to prevent Cleveland from falling into default on its bonds. The crisis of Cleveland was a long time brewing, but the search for an answer fell into the lap of newly elected Mayor Dennis Kucinich, a former city councilman. Kucinich was born in Cleveland shortly after World War Two, which was about when the city's troubles began. In the succeeding decades, the city was filled with poor whites and blacks migrating from the South, looking for jobs. As happened in so many other cities, the middle and upper classes began to flee to the suburbs. Mortgages were hard to come by. The inner city and the tax base shrank.

Kucinich, the council, and the banks squared off in a three-way battle. None would give an inch. Reportedly, the banks demanded the sale of the city's public Municipal Light System (Muny) before they would roll over the notes the city needed to keep afloat. Rokakis points out that some board members of the banks that refused to roll over the loans also sat on the board of the city's private utility, Cleveland Electric Illuminating Company (CEI), and had a vested interest in forcing the city to sell Muny. (Cleveland is now in the midst of an antitrust case against the private utility, charging that it tried to undermine Muny; CEI's own attorneys have disclosed in the trial that, among other things, the utility had brought lawsuits against Muny in an effort to harass the smaller company.)

Rokakis, who had been active in battles against utility rate hikes since high school, strongly supported Kucinich's refusal to hand the system over to CEI, which provides most of the city's light. "I feel Muny is probably the most valuable asset the city has, not to mention its symbolic value," Rokakis says. "It is incumbent upon us to make Muny . . . a viable source of energy for people in the Cleveland area." When the banks refused to support the city, Kucinich went on the nightly news and invited Cleveland residents to withdraw their money from Cleveland Trust. Rokakis would have joined the mayor in protest, except, he says, "I didn't have any money in the bank." Running a campaign had eaten up his savings. Kucinich did not have much either, and his symbolic move did not change the bank's position. On December 15, when Kucinich said no to the request to sell Muny, Cleveland Trust called in the loans and Cleveland fell.

Saving Cleveland came down to either selling Muny or raising income taxes. Cleveland residents apparently shared Rokakis and Kucinich's view about the importance of retaining ownership of Muny—they voted in a general election to raise their income taxes and to keep Muny in the city's hands. After two years, Cleveland was on firm financial footing once again. In addition, Muny has added a second interconnect, which ensures its forty thousand customers that if one interconnect fails, they will not be without power, as they would have in the past. Rokakis says the utility is preparing to expand its service to additional customers over the next few years.

In 1979, when Rokakis ran again for city council, he won with a whopping 74 percent of the vote—and that was against the former council member from the district. In 1981, council districts changed, and in addition to his working-class neighborhoods, Rokakis was running in middle- and upper-class areas. He got 81 percent of the vote in his old neighborhood and won the overall race with 55 percent.

Though the city has recovered from bankruptcy, it has not recovered from the general decline facing most northeastern, industrialized cities. As old industry dies, its high-tech counterpart has not moved into cities such as Cleveland to provide jobs and revenue. And while Rokakis is reviewing actions he can take through the city council to create jobs in Cleveland (unemployment stands at 20 percent), he is also passing legislation to address problems such as arson, pay inequity between men and women, and utility shutoffs to low-income tenants. Rokakis is also sponsoring a "community right to know" ordinance, which would force companies producing hazardous material to alert their workers and surrounding communities to the health effects and exposure limits of the substance. In addition, Rokakis is proposing a law that would limit the Cleveland police department's use of covert intelligence-gathering activities. Rokakis said the department in past years has had detectives following alleged "subversives," from Dr. Benjamin Spock (the "baby doctor," peace activist, and professor at Case Western Reserve) to members of local black organizations and Jane Fonda, when she has been in Cleveland.

Rokakis notes that he is the only council member to introduce progressive legislation in the past five years. But the council is becoming more active, and he adds, "people in council are giving the city a more progressive image."

Rokakis admits that many people in his district may feel some of the issues he is promoting are removed from their day-to-day lives. The dog next door barks too much, neighborhood boys playing football in the street are breaking car windows, the garbage collectors spill trash when they make their pick-up; these are the things residents look to the council to handle. "Not everyone sees the big picture—how these other issues [like toxic and radioactive wastes] affect their lives," Rokakis says. That is why he has continued the newsletter: to inform his constituents about the work he is doing and what it means for them. On top of all this activity with the council, Rokakis also completed an earlier goal: law school. He attended night courses at Cleveland State Law School, and finished in four years. But he has no plans to go off to a law practice. He has too many ideas for Cleveland and they will be accomplished from the inside, not the outside. His usually spirited discussion of the problems and progress in Cleveland's past becomes even more animated when he talks about Cleveland's future.

"In spite of all this city's miserable misfortune, over the

past five years the neighborhoods have stabilized," he notes. Neighborhoods are his focal point; he wants to promote small businesses and jobs in the city to prevent people from moving to the suburbs. He wants to establish job training programs for unemployed steelworkers and others. Then he wants to attract high-tech industry to the depressed area. Why would they move to Cleveland? It goes back to the city's neighborhoods: "You can get a huge Victorian house for twenty-five thousand dollars," Rokakis says.

At thirty, with only four members having served more time than Rokakis on the twenty-three-member council, he has a lot of opportunity to have an impact on the city. When asked what his goals are he pauses, starts to answer, then pauses again. One begins to wonder if he is about to confess to having political aspirations that will lead him away from the city he is so committed to now. So what about those goals? "I'm doing some of what I want to do on the city council . . . but the real power is in the mayor's office. I have to say I would like to be mayor of Cleveland."

## MARSHA GOMBERG

When Marsha Gomberg was growing up in Los Angeles, she envied her older brother and her parents. They were active participants in antiwar rallies and civil rights marches, but she was too young to be involved. Still, their activism during the height of those efforts left an impression on her.

So, when she began college in 1978, she took with her a strong concern about issues her parents and brother wrestled with: the environment, consumer fraud, social justice. But, she figured, the days of student activism were gone, and there would be no meaningful way to address those concerns as a student at Lewis and Clark College in Oregon.

It did not take long for Gomberg to discover she was wrong.

Gomberg got involved in a variety of activities during her first year of college—from student government committees to staffing a rape crisis hotline. As a dorm resident, she also took part in the activities of the residents' association. It was through the dorm that she was introduced to Oregon Student PIRG (OSPIRG). A couple of friends were working on an OSPIRG survey of local doctors to determine whether they would take Medicaid patients. Gomberg was enlisted to play the role of a potential patient. She called doctors to see if they would accept her as a Medicaid recipient. From there, Gomberg began sitting in on OSPIRG meetings and discussing ways to involve students. Gomberg took the lead in developing plans to expand the student base, mostly through projects on landlord/tenant issues, health care surveys, and campus workshops to teach students about other OSPIRG issues. At its May meeting, the five-member state board elected her chairperson.

"I fell into OSPIRG backwards, and the next thing I knew I was elected to the board," Gomberg says.

OSPIRG was looking for new issues and more members. The staff was small, but it still churned out reports on everything from forest protection to juvenile detention practices. The student who did the juvenile justice study was appointed to a governor's commission on juvenile detention as a result of the report, but that accomplishment, along with other OSPIRG successes, was not widely known on the campuses. This concerned Gomberg. She was convinced that OSPIRG could double its effectiveness by informing students about its accomplishments and stepping up recruitment.

Being new to Oregon and to the organization, Gomberg was not aware of OSPIRG's track record or what PIRGs at other campuses across the nation had done. She might have been content with the low-profile of OSPIRG, assuming it was just a sign of the times. But then a local newspaper reporter encouraged her: "OSPIRG has a vibrant history. You've got to continue the tradition."

Gomberg began making contact with former OSPIRG staff and students, and with PIRG organizers and staff in other states. She attended a national PIRG conference, where she learned about the work other PIRGs were doing and how they faced similar problems. Veteran organizers such as Donald Ross, who had helped students set up the first PIRG in Oregon seven years earlier, helped Gomberg design a campaign to make OSPIRG more visible. Convinced that students were victims of a lack of information about OSPIRG rather than of apathy, "I became interested in relating OSPIRG's good issue work to Oregon students," Gomberg says. "Once we rallied people around the issues, we had tremendous student involvement."

That fall, OSPIRG staff and students spoke in classrooms and before campus groups explaining what the PIRG had been doing and what it could do if more students got involved. Sixty students from across the state attended a series of workshops on organizing, lobbying, and research. The PIRG held conferences for students on issues it had been researching, such as forest and water preservation, landlord/tenant rights, and banking and medical services.

By the next spring, OSPIRG had expanded onto two more campuses and created a thirty-person state board. Campus chapters came alive with students investigating spraying of the carcinogenic herbicide 2,4,5-T, finding doctors to testify before legislators about its health effects, and forging a coalition of community groups to monitor the spraying of the herbicide to make sure it was not done carelessly. They studied nursing homes in the state and wrote a popular report on the variety of services homes offer and the regulations governing them. The state Department of Human Resources Office of Elderly Affairs said in a letter to OSPIRG, "This guide offers in one concise volume much valuable information for both residents and concerned citizens."

Gomberg and others were also interested in preserving the state's rich natural environment. OSPIRG supported a bill protecting wilderness areas that eventually became law. With a $56,000 grant from the National Science Foundation, OSPIRG indexed trees and wildlife existing in Oregon forest areas to help determine if they should be protected as wilderness.

After her sophomore year as state board chair, Gomberg went to Portugal for a year of study. When she returned to Lewis and Clark, she was drawn back to OSPIRG—her last year of college revolved around promoting the PIRG on campuses and organizing PIRG projects.

After college, Gomberg went home to California and took a summer job with State Senator Alan Sieroty, where she worked on child care issues, education, and historical preservation. Gomberg says her OSPIRG work helped prepare her for the position. "I think employers are excited anytime someone is involved in projects that complement the classroom activities," Gomberg says.

After working for the senator, Gomberg received a nine-month Coro Foundation Fellowship. The Coro Foundation internship allows people to work in several sectors of society—business, labor, government, community, and political organizations. The inside view she got of these sectors helped her "see how complicated the world is. I had thought it was all bad guys and good guys." While the internship allowed her to see issues from all sides, she says, "It didn't encourage me to water down my opinions. I have the same ideals, but I am also more interested in learning about the other side and understanding what I'm up against."

It is a lesson she began learning at OSPIRG. "There is a balance between painting issues simplistically to get support, and doing quality, in-depth work," she says.

When she completed the Coro internship, Gomberg worked with a company that produces documentaries for cable television. She produced an award-winning series on a special educational program in a low-income area of Los Angeles. The production focused on an elementary school where the children's instruction includes dances and crafts from other cultures. In the project's junior high school, students learn computer programming and how to use computers for accounting and other projects. In the high school, known mostly for its athletes and street gangs, some teachers provide special assistance to students wishing to go to college in a program called College Corps. Because of that program, more students were applying, and getting accepted, to college. Gomberg found one student who had attended all three schools. She had him host the series.

The series won first place in the National Federation of Local Cable Programmers' documentary division, and the schools are using it to inform interested students and parents about the program.

After completing the video project in the latter part of 1982, Gomberg's interest in urban and rural development led her and a friend to take six months to travel around the world, particularly in India, to "get a better understanding of how the world works." She lived on a kibbutz in Israel, visited tribal villages and "pavement schools" in the streets of India, and even met with then Prime Minister Indira Gandhi.

Now that she is back in the United States, Gomberg sees the need to reach audiences that have not been reached before. The documentary she did on the educational program was just the beginning; she began a job in October 1983 with WNET in New York as an assistant to the editor of a weekly educational program aimed at high school students called "Why in the World." Gomberg likes to provide people with information about issues—especially people who do not have easy access to the information. "It is something that started with my work at OSPIRG," she says.

When Gomberg looks through her parents' scrapbook and sees them photographed at such events as the 1963 March on Washington, the massive civil rights rally at which Martin Luther King, Jr., gave his famous "I have a dream" speech, she regrets that activist students of her era had to spend so much time battling apathy. It was frustrating, at times—organizing students in the seventies was hard. There was not the visible, widespread support for causes that students of the sixties had displayed. PIRG work may not always compare with the high drama of civil rights efforts and intense demonstrations, but, she says, "It's a start. It is meaningful in and of itself. It is an important part of a person's college education."

## KARIM AHMED

It is surprising to some people that a postdoctorate fellow in medical school would take time to pay attention to anything other than demanding studies. Yet Karim Ahmed, like many other students, was concerned about many things beyond the walls of his classrooms. In 1971, he decided to act on his concerns, and began organizing a PIRG at the University of Minnesota. He forged a path that many other PIRG activists would follow, blending a science-oriented education with public interest work on a wide range of environmental issues that required a scientific background.

Today, as a scientist familiar with lobbying, fundraising, and administration of a nonprofit organization, Ahmed is a good example of what a public interest advocate with an advanced degree in natural sciences can do.

Like so many people in the seventies, Ahmed was concerned about ecological threats and he wanted to do something about them. He began meeting with some people in the community with similar concerns, but they had not established any sort of vehicle for addressing those concerns. In the fall of 1971, during a speech at the University of Minnesota, Ralph Nader explained the PIRG concept, and Ahmed thought it sounded like a good idea. Nader associate Donald Ross came to Minnesota to help develop a funding base, and local attorney Allan Saeks, who had worked with Nader in Washington, D.C., advised the student PIRG organizers.

Since this was one of the first efforts to set up a PIRG on campus, the methods were not clearly defined. Ahmed remembers thinking that getting support for the PIRG with a petition drive would not work. An antiwar petition during the height of the Vietnam War had produced only ten thousand signatures on that year's campus of forty-two thousand. But Ahmed was wrong. In just two weeks, petitioners for Minnesota PIRG (MPIRG) got thirty thousand signatures—nearly 60 percent of the campus—at the University of Minnesota. On other campuses, petitioners were successful too. "The timing was right," Ahmed says in a clear understatement. Within the first year, MPIRG was established at virtually all colleges and universities in the state.

With funding in place, the PIRG hired Chuck Dayton as its senior attorney. Dayton left his position as partner in a large Minneapolis law firm to take the PIRG position; he also took about a $15,000 cut in pay. In another understatement, Ahmed says of Dayton: "He was a very seasoned attorney."

At this point Ahmed figured his future with PIRG would be as an advisor on organizing matters. He had finished his postdoctorate fellowship and was considering an offer to continue research at the medical school. Ahmed, however, became MPIRG's first research director, guiding students through extensive projects to provide background for MPIRG legal cases or as the basis of MPIRG reports.

When he took the PIRG position instead of pursuing academic research in his field, Ahmed knew he was going to be applying his skills in a much less abstract way than his colleagues. He also knew he was not taking the prescribed course for a career in academia as he had planned. But once he became involved in MPIRG research full time, he says, it became clear to him that he did not want to follow the established scientific career path.

So, with the likes of Ahmed heading up research projects, Dayton and Saeks providing advice and legal advocacy, and hundreds of students doing research and writing, MPIRG quickly became a successful public interest group. It took determination. "It was an eighteen-hour-a-day job. Weekends, weekdays, you couldn't tell the difference," Ahmed recalls. Besides devising and supervising research projects, Ahmed testified before the legislature on MPIRG initiatives and continued to help chapters organize or renegotiate contracts.

MPIRG worked on tenants' rights, banking issues, toy safety, and more. In 1972, MPIRG also conducted an extensive study on the health effects of asbestos. The study focused on the lax procedures for handling the material on and near construction sites. The PIRG's work led the legislature to prohibit the use of asbestos as building insulation. Most environmental groups haven't had such impressive beginnings, Ahmed says. But then he adds, most haven't had as many professionals working with an active membership.

After two years as MPIRG's research director, Ahmed was offered a job with Consumers Union in New York. He was thirty-two years old, with a wife and two kids—the $25,000 salary was enticing and the work would still be serving the public interest. But Ahmed hesitated; "I had worked so hard to get the organization off the ground, I felt like it would leave them in a lurch." Dayton had gone on to start his own law practice, and since he and Ahmed had been acting as co-directors, if Ahmed left there would be no one to direct the organization. So Ahmed stayed long enough to help find an executive director. Then, when he was satisfied the PIRG had the resources and momentum to maintain itself, he left for New York.

After a year as executive assistant to the executive director of Consumer Union, Ahmed became head of the Natural Resources Defense Council (NRDC) science program. Ahmed says his knowledge of the legislature and public policy is what made him a good candidate for both positions. "Every time we hire a scientist," he says, "we ask the applicants if they've done work with local community or public interest groups." But often the response is "very discouraging," he says, because most applicants have limited experience in public policy work, and are naive about how decisions are made in the political arena. A scientist with a Ph.D. who has no experience with community groups or volunteer work will probably not even be considered for a job at NRDC, he says.

As head of NRDC's science program, Ahmed does a lot of public speaking, testifying, and meeting with officials of industry and government. He says, "I learned to be quick on my feet; when someone throws a curve ball, I have to be able to hit it." It is something he never would have learned if he had become a "dyed-in-the-wool, narrowly trained" scientist instead of working for PIRG.

Even compared with eight years of academic study, Ahmed says, "The two years with PIRG were as much of a learning experience as I've had in my life." He had not realized he had the skill to interest people in an issue and motivate them to take action, or to testify before a legislative committee. "I was a very studious undergrad in physics. But in PIRG I found out I had more political savvy than I thought I did," Ahmed says.

When Ahmed made the decision to work full time for MPIRG instead of doing research at the medical school, he knew it would change the direction of his career. He had planned to go into teaching and do public interest work part time. Now, he is teaching a single course in toxicology and environmental science at the State University of New York; academics have taken the part-time role. "I guess PIRG sort of turned things around for me," he laughs. "Now I'm doing full-time public interest work and part-time teaching."

At the time, Ahmed was a little concerned about whether he had made the right decision in leaving behind a full-fledged career as a professor and researcher. But now, he says, "I don't see it as a sacrifice. . . . It suits me fine."

# SEVEN

# PIRGs: Action and Reaction

Every PIRG project brings important benefits to the students who carry it forward. Tom Ryan, former director of Missouri PIRG, notes his business and law degrees, but then says confidently, "The best education I have received has been working with PIRG." Ryan, who organized MOPIRG in 1972 and worked there until 1985, would agree with another native of the Show-Me State, Mark Twain, who advised, "Don't let your studies get in the way of your education."

Ryan's statement is not an exception; many people who have worked in PIRGs will respond the same way—"I've learned more in what I did with PIRG than I did in any class"—if you ask them whether the PIRG experience was educational. It may not even be fair to compare the two. For example, no textbook description of the legislative process can capture the drama of committee hearings that turn to shouting matches or of students being able to change the minds of strong-willed opponents. Debating a topic before a class cannot match the excitement and importance of rebutting false claims an opponent makes to a legislator. Seeing a well-researched letter to the editor printed in a newspaper gives more meaning to a writing project than knowing that a paper just sits in some professor's temporary files.

In addition, as former NYPIRG Project Coordinator Sharon Neuman says, "People who take on a PIRG project see they can do things competently. They realize they can do more than read books to do well on tests."

Not that PIRGs don't put students' ability to the test. From organizing a chapter on campus to lobbying a bill through the legislature, students know that if their effort fails, it means more than an "F" on an exam. Consider a college theater group: What if they cast roles for a magnificent play and then only rehearsed the lines but never performed it for anyone? The rehearsals would be worthwhile to strengthen the actors' skills, but what if there never was any promise of using those skills to perform for an audience? The theater company would probably dwindle away. PIRGs allow students to perform the roles of advocate, organizer, writer, or researcher in the outside world—roles they may have only read about or discussed in classes. Since students are able to take that extra step, universities see PIRG projects as an extension of the classroom work, and students receive academic credit for their work.

Joseph Murphy, chancellor of the City University of New York, has been a long-time supporter of the PIRGs, and he sees them as playing an important role in students' education. "PIRGs are a very effective vehicle to involve students in citizen action," Murphy says. Since PIRGs work in the courts, the legislature, and the community, students learn far more about the world around them than they would with strictly campus-based groups such as student government. "It is important for students to see there can be a correlation between political action and positive outcome," Murphy says. Realizing that they can have an impact leads students to take their role as citizens seriously, a vital aspect of a democracy, he notes.

Political science is one of the departments most likely to view PIRG work as an application of what is learned in the classroom. Going beyond theories about what makes people take an interest in the political system or how a bill travels through Congress, students participate in voter-education drives or take a bill, from scratch, through the entire legislative process. While a professor can lecture about the relationship of government regulators to other branches of government, when students monitor the actions of an agency to see whether it is complying with legislative mandates, they concretely understand the powers and responsibilities of each area.

Elaborate public opinion surveys conducted by students through PIRGs often earn students course credit in sociology; economic analysis of a utility rate increase or new plant construction earns credit in economics or mathematics. In cases where projects don't qualify for full course credit, the reports students write or research can often be used to fulfill requirements for research papers with a regular class; food or other product surveys can meet part of the requirements for a consumer economics course.

A special program at Boston College, called the Pulse Program, combines academic study with social service and advocacy work. It gives students credit for working with a community group, such as Massachusetts Association for the Blind, Cambridge-Somerville Mental Health, Friends of the Elderly, Boston Legal Services, and MASSPIRG. Pulse Program Director Dick Keeley says the aspect of PIRG that makes it a vital part of the program is "PIRG's emphasis on addressing problems systematically, and teaching students to attack problems of injustices." Keeley adds that MASSPIRG also provides students with something none of the other agencies in Pulse provide—an inside view of the complexities of the legislative system.

Some universities do not have such a well-defined

program for giving credit for such extracurricular activities. In that case, the first step someone who plans to work with PIRG can take is to talk with professors and propose doing the project for independent study credits. The student can explain what he or she will work on, and how it fits within a discipline, and then plan a schedule for completing the project. For example, a student in Alaska got independent study credit when he surveyed Teamsters Union members. AKPIRG assembled a few students to work on the survey, and gained access to university resources for compiling the data. In the end, the student received course credit, and the survey and AKPIRG received national media attention when Walter Cronkite presented the survey results as part of a *CBS News* report on teamsters.

Going through the process of convincing a professor or administrator that a project is applicable to a certain subject and is worth course credit serves as an introduction to the kinds of skills a student will learn by working with PIRG: documenting a position, advocating it, and moving it through the proper channels. Also, professors may be persuaded to support a student's work when they see the student is willing to take the initiative to learn beyond the classroom.

Participating in a PIRG project not only provides people with new skills, it often gives them a new perspective on their role in society. Indeed, it was one of the things Ralph Nader had in mind when he encouraged students to get involved beyond the campus. Nader recognized that the vast majority of Americans are not given many opportunities to learn the skills needed to participate effectively in the political system. Once people learned those skills and were able to have an impact with them, he reasoned, they could not ignore their new-found power, so they would continue to be active participants in the system. Their part-time role would be a firm base of support for those who choose to make full-time careers of public interest work. PIRG projects can provide valuable opportunities and experiences for all students, no matter what their particular field of study. Let's say students are studying art and plan to illustrate children's books for a living. They do not need the upper-level credit in the economics or political science department they might get from working with PIRG; they might think keeping abreast of current events and going to the polls is about as active as they need to be in "politics." Why would they want to learn the skills a PIRG teaches? "Because everyone decides to live in a town where there are local problems," answers former PIRG student and staff member Bob Chlopak. "In that town they will confront unjust property taxes or rent increases, but without basic knowledge of the system they will be victimized," he continues. "Having spent time confronting those issues through PIRG will allow them to improve the quality of their own life when it is undermined."

Besides, PIRGs can use the help of students in all fields of study. The citizen groups need artists to design displays, brochures, and other publications, and art students can expand their portfolios with such work. Business, marketing, foreign languages, accounting, natural sciences, communications—students in any of these disciplines can provide vital assistance to a PIRG, and gain skills that are applicable to their field.

In addition to teaching students how to grapple with countless issues around them, PIRG projects provide people in the community with examples of advocacy techniques. Aside from students' action in the community, PIRG handbooks, special-topic brochures, and newsletters are designed to create a citizenry that is more informed of its rights and more involved in community issues. The range of topics and distribution of these publications is far-reaching.

The mainstay of PIRG literature is its regular magazine, which keeps students and members of the community abreast of the PIRG's issues. New York PIRG's news magazine, *Agenda for Citizen Involvement*, Minnesota PIRG's *StateWatch*, Missouri PIRG's *MOPIRG Reports*, and Colorado PIRG's *Colorado Outlook* are examples of the professional, informative nature of these PIRG publications. These newsletters contain articles explaining the issues and the ways citizens can get involved. They also advise readers about legislators' voting records, PIRG studies, and civic information.

In addition, many PIRGs publish guides to important services so consumers can make the comparison that will save them money and help ensure quality. The PIRGs in Michigan and Maryland have published useful guides explaining how to select doctors and other medical services. The New Mexico PIRG offers a guide to women's health care, and Ohio PIRG provides information in both English and Spanish about how to get free medical care. PIRGs in North Carolina, New York, and Missouri have published directories to prescription drugs.

Many PIRG handbooks seek to explain the bureaucracies that people are often reluctant to use because of their seeming complexity. Several PIRGs have published small-claims-court guides telling how to file cases and assemble necessary information for a case, and what to expect even after the case is finished. Others offer directions for using a state's freedom-of-information act (FOIA) to obtain government agency documents. In some places, it has been more than a matter of teaching people how to use a FOIA. The Peterborough and Waterloo chapters of Ontario PIRG had the task of explaining why freedom-of-information laws were needed in Canada; their report examined the entrenched secrecy in Canadian government and, using the FOIAs of countries such as the United States and Sweden as examples, discussed what must be included in the legislation to make it effective.

PIRGs also publish guides such as NYPIRG's "How to Complain About Your Lawyer" and manuals for holding conferences and teach-ins on energy issues like nuclear power and solar alternatives.

Probably the most popular type of PIRG publications are the "Know Your Rights" guides, directed at specific segments of society. The guides examine the problems those people are likely to face and give advice about what legal rights they have. PIRGs in Minnesota and Missouri have printed handbooks on women's rights; in Minnesota and Iowa, on the rights of the elderly. By far the most common handbook on rights is the one for tenants. Virtually all PIRGs have published booklets or at least brochures on this issue. Minnesota PIRG's tenants' rights handbook is in its sixth printing with more than thirty thousand copies distributed in English and Spanish. The handbooks outline what a tenant needs to know about leases, security deposits, complaint procedures, eviction, and steps for legal recourse. Missouri PIRG's handbook also contains step-by-step advice on how to organize a tenants' association. Tenants' rights booklets are popular with students, most of whom are first-time renters, and with nonstudent renters.

As offshoots of the services that publications provide, PIRGs often staff complaint centers, such as NYPIRG's on the Educational Testing Service. Through complaint centers, examples of fraud or recurrent problems with a service or product are often discovered.

Another PIRG service is the hotline. Connecticut PIRG, like several others, has for years trained student interns to staff its hotlines. Using manuals developed by CONNPIRG, the interns are able to provide consumers with answers to their questions or refer them to the appropriate source.

The Iowa PIRG has a similar operation that participated in an extensive investigation of the Student Health Service at Iowa State. Iowa PIRG's Consumer Protection Service received more than seventy complaints about one doctor at the Health Services Gynecology Clinic. The PIRG met with the director of student health to ensure that only students who requested that gynecologist would be treated by him. In addition, the government of the student body passed a resolution in support of Iowa PIRG, calling for the suspension of the doctor and calling for representatives from Iowa PIRG to be included on the selection committee for a new doctor.

It was a Maryland PIRG tenants' hotline, run in conjunction with neighborhood associations, that led to a tense confrontation for a PIRG student volunteer. Some landlords in the Washington, D.C., area tried to bypass the legal safeguards against sudden tenant eviction. Getting rid of the family in an apartment opens up the potential for bringing in a new family—at substantially higher rent. A tight housing market will often encourage this practice. After taking a call on the hotline from a group of tenants in just that situation, MARYPIRG volunteer Stephanie Triplett decided to take a first-hand look at the problem.

She saw a group hired by the landlord, backed by a crew of sheriff's deputies, preparing to haul away the tenants' belongings. Some of the tenants had found eviction notices posted on their door only the night before. But as Triplett quickly discovered, the landlord had not obtained the court orders necessary for eviction. Armed with that knowledge, the residents began an ad-hoc resistance, plopping children on furniture to keep it from being moved, barricading doors, and moving throughout the building to gather support. And after Triplett made a few quick phone calls, the bright lights of the TV cameras arrived and the illegal eviction the landlord had planned was squelched. Faced with a chanting cordon of residents, and with TV cameras recording his every move, the landlord backed down. The deputies and the moving crew turned and left, without evicting any of the families.

From this beginning, the building's residents have continued to work together, learning, according to Triplett, many "legal intricacies." Their new power, she adds, has helped to prevent further abuse, and it has given Triplett, who stepped in at the crucial moment, a sense of real accomplishment.

PIRG's involvement with the community, then, has brought its residents some valuable services, but more importantly, it has given people the opportunity to discover what citizenship is all about. They learn that they *can* have an impact on the workings of government and private industry. PIRGs have always known they would need support in the community to accomplish many of their goals, so they have developed that support by building coalitions through grass-roots community organizing.

One of the more recent—and heartwarming—examples began in April 1985, when PIRGs across the country, in cooperation with USA for Africa, launched the National Student Campaign Against Hunger. Both groups were seeking to broaden the concern that had been tapped by the song "We Are the World."

Working with other student groups, hunger groups, and USA for Africa, the campaign established a national speaker's bureau to increase awareness of the extent of hunger both abroad and at home. In addition, the campaign helped set up standing committees on hunger at ten campuses. The committees have organized food salvage programs with campus dining services and have set up numerous city- and statewide hunger programs with other colleges. Finally, the group joined Hands Across

America, sponsoring recruitment projects on campuses for the line, and helping local activists sponsor "line segments" across their campus or city. On May 25, 1986, students joined with millions of other Americans in the largest participatory event in human history, linking hands to demonstrate commitment to ending domestic hunger.

Coalition building is a natural development for PIRGs. Generous with student and staff time and possessing no ideological quirks that would bar cooperation with other groups, PIRGs have worked with a large number of independent and public organizations. By being nonpartisan, PIRGs can find broad-based support, which means their efforts will be more successful. It allows them to address the full range of student needs and interests with a strong voice. Minnesota's PIRG, for example, has sponsored conferences, supported legislative items, and advanced projects in conjunction with the Sierra Club, Izaak Walton League, Northern States Power Co., AFL-CIO, Minnesota Trial Lawyers, Minnesota Senior Citizens Association, and various churches in the state. Shown that MPIRG has the backing of that variety of groups, public officials could hardly discount its proposals as coming from "just a bunch of kids."

The North Carolina PIRG and Missouri PIRG worked with labor unions on worker health, safety, and compensation issues; NYPIRG worked with senior citizens' and hearing-impaired groups along with audiologists on hearing aid sales reform; the Oregon PIRG brought together groups of senior citizens, environmentalists, taxpayers, and ratepayers to win the initiative campaign to create a citizens' utility board.

Veteran PIRG organizer C.B. Pearson explains, "Enter any state where there is a PIRG and you'll find the organization well known among other citizen groups. PIRG students and staff are great coalition builders."

Adds Karen Burstein, head of New York's Civil Service

Commission, "Anyone who is a consumer activist in the state of New York is aligned with NYPIRG."

Beyond aligning themselves with PIRGs, in some cases groups of individuals will realize the need to start their own group that may be able to give more time to an issue than PIRG can; a PIRG staff member or student volunteer may even become involved in forming the group. Oregon's Student PIRG, for example, was instrumental in the formation of an Oregon environmental group called the "1000 Friends of Oregon." In 1970 and 1971, law student Henry Richmond was active in the original OSPIRG organizing effort, and after graduating and clerking for a federal judge for a year, Richmond joined the OSPIRG staff as an attorney. Richmond worked for OSPIRG from 1972 through 1975. His work focused on the Oregon state land use program set up by the 1973 Oregon legislature. Richmond supervised two influential OSPIRG reports, one on soil types and prime farm land, and the other on Oregon estuaries. Both these reports offered recommendations for potential regulations for the new state land use agency, many of which were adopted.

By that time, it was apparent to Richmond that an opposition force of real estate people, builders, forest product companies, and short-sighted local officials could prevent the new laws from being properly administered. Richmond believed that an entire organization was needed to ensure that land use legislation was enforced, so he and others moved to create 1000 Friends for that purpose. They put together a funding base by gaining pledges of $100 per year from a number of individuals (the "1000 Friends") and Richmond left OSPIRG in the spring of 1975 to become the new group's director. By mid-1980, 1000 Friends had filed more than five hundred memos and briefs with local government offices concerning the implementation of the land use act and had filed over fifty lawsuits—winning in more than 90 percent of the cases.

"There was a continued connection between OSPIRG and 1000 Friends," Richmond said, pointing out that OSPIRG's first director, Steven McCarthy, sits on the 1000 Friends Board of Directors and 1000 Friends staff attorneys had previously served as OSPIRG interns while in law school.

Other groups spun off from PIRGs include the Brown Lung Association in North Carolina, which got its start when NCPIRG fought for better protection for textile workers susceptible to the disease. The BLA is active in a four-state region, picking up worker and community education efforts on the issue while NCPIRG moves on to other projects. In New York, NYPIRG formed a Citizens Alliance to give the PIRG a community base. The Citizens Alliance recently became independent of NYPIRG. As these groups become independent, they still are part of the broad base of community support PIRGs have developed over the years.

However, from the vantage point of a utility company executive, owner of a polluting industrial plant, or other businessperson, PIRG participation is not always welcome. Utility operators know that, in some cases, a PIRG is about all that stands between the stockholders and higher profits, while polluters often find that PIRGs are pointing a well-researched finger at them to force compliance with air standards. Or worse, PIRGs are working to amend laws for stricter air standards, and have sought to educate employees about their rights to a safe workplace. The local funeral director who only made available his most expensive services to his bereaved customers finds that PIRG has sought reform that prevents his profitable but unfair sales practices. The services and products of auto repair shops and supermarkets will not escape scrutiny from enthusiastic PIRG researchers, who, if they find problems, will make them public. Landlords find that PIRGs have made tenants more knowledgeable about their rights, and legislators look around in their district and learn that their constituents have been keeping a PIRG's-eye view of activities in the state capitol.

These are not pleasant revelations for those who may be at the wrong end of a documented PIRG report, or draw the ire of PIRG-activated citizenry. As PIRGs grow in strength and scope, it stands to reason that there will be some attempts to weaken the organization. The most favored technique is to attack the PIRG student funding mechanism. Critics of PIRG's work charge that the democratically selected funding means—usually a waivable fee included on the tuition bill—is unfair and inconvenient to those who do not want to support PIRGs. Their alleged concern for students having to pay fees to organizations they do not support does not extend to the nonrefundable student service fees used for everything from athletics to art, however.

Detractors have used a variety of means, including lawsuits, to try to weaken or abolish PIRGs altogether. In New Jersey, eight students, represented by the Mid-Atlantic Legal Foundation (MALF), filed suit against Rutgers University and the New Jersey PIRG. The suit claimed the PIRG's fee collection violated their constitutional rights. So, in 1979, not satisfied with their refund, the students took the matter to court. The legal foundation representing them is funded by such corporations as Chase-Manhattan Bank, Exxon Co. USA, U.S. Steel Foundation, and Atlantic Richfield Foundation. The plaintiffs argued that using part of students' activity fees to fund an organization involved in civic issues was infringing on a student's right not to affiliate with that ideology. While the attack was aimed at the PIRG, and at the administration for allowing it to be funded, the suit was widely seen as an attack on activism in general. As NYPIRG Executive Director Tom Wathen noted in a letter to *The New York*

*Times*, "[These lawsuits] threaten to unravel efforts made by students and educators alike to teach students the skills they will need to uphold a governmental process that requires an active citizenry."

New York Assemblyman William Passannante headed a 1969 Legislative Commission on Campus Unrest. He maintains now, as he did then, that students have a right to use their money as they see fit. "I've seen all that [protests and rallies of the sixties] turn into a very positive, working effort," Passannante says. "PIRGs are one of the most positive things that came out of the sixties unrest."

In 1984, NJPIRG won a favorable ruling in the case, *Galda* (Joseph Galda, one of the students) v. *Bloustein* (Edward J. Bloustein, president of Rutgers). U.S. District Court Judge Stanley Brotman said in his opinion that "PIRG has a very substantial educational component, and its presence at Rutgers significantly enhances the educational opportunities available for students [there]." Brotman's decision, however, was overturned the following year by the U.S. Third Circuit Court of Appeals. The principal problem with the challenged funding mechanism, said the court, is that it created a special external vehicle—unique to PIRG—for collecting the PIRG fee.

Although the decision was a disappointment for NJPIRG, the court went out of its way to note that almost any funding vehicle that doesn't compel students to contribute to PIRG involuntarily, however temporarily, would be acceptable.

In March 1986, the U.S. Supreme Court let the appeals court decision stand by declining to hear an appeal brought by Rutgers and NJPIRG. As a result, as noted earlier, a waivable fee, akin to that in other public colleges, is now in place at Rutgers.

A similar case was filed by MALF in February 1983 for eight New York students against the New York PIRG. MALF is suing the State University of New York (SUNY)

Board of Trustees and the presidents of three SUNY campuses, along with NYPIRG, on grounds similar to those in the New Jersey case.

An important distinction between the two cases is that the New York PIRG is funded through the regular student fee mechanism, and is treated just like the chess club, the football team, and other student programs. Although the New York case has yet to be tried, lawyers for NYPIRG and SUNY are confident that this distinction will weigh heavily in favor of PIRG.

Two other groups organizing a campaign against PIRGs are the College Republicans and a group calling itself Young Americans for Freedom. The College Republican National Committee distributed an "anti-PIRG packet" that suggests ways to disrupt PIRG activities and to try to get other campus groups to oppose PIRG. It also suggests threatening university administrators with legal action if PIRGs are allowed to stay in place.

Ignoring bipartisan support on PIRG bills and broad-based community support, these groups characterize PIRGs as "leftist" organizations. Their other unsuccessful means of attacking the PIRGs are to get elected to local and then state PIRG boards and try to dismantle the group from within, or to advocate legislation that would restrict the ways in which student fees can be used.

In Florida, a member of the College Republicans urged a state representative to sponsor legislation that would make the refusable/refundable fee illegal. The refusable/refundable, or negative check-off, means that the $2.50 fee is added to a student's tuition unless he or she refuses it by marking a space on the registration form, or asks for a refund at any time during the semester. The student who opposed the fee said the process was undemocratic, despite the fact it was put in place after a majority of the students signed petitions, the board of regents approved the system, and the presidents of the universities okayed the refusable/refundable fee.

College Republican organizations on other Florida campuses charged the PIRG with involvement in controversial issues. Florida PIRG's activities have included publishing a handbook on landlord/tenant law, hosting three environmental conferences, researching the problem of toxic wastes, staffing consumer/tenant hotlines, and supporting a "lemon law" that enforces new car warranties.

Florida PIRG students and staff countered by writing letters to their representatives, and sought endorsements from campus organizations, faculty members, and administrators. Several student and city newspapers editorialized in favor of Florida PIRG and its funding. A group of fourteen representatives to the statehouse wrote a letter to the Board of Regents of the State University System in support of FPIRG, saying, "It is very important to Florida's future that its Universities turn out as many civic-minded individuals, grounded in democratic principles, as possible. Florida PIRG will instill these values in . . . individuals." The Florida Board of Regents had agreed with that concept when it granted its approval of the PIRG funding system after several months of studying it. Betty Ann Stant, vice-chairperson of the board, told *The Florida Flambeau* newspaper, "It seems to me that [Florida PIRG] is a good way for the students to take a more active part in the democratic process." The measure to undermine PIRG failed.

A Florida regent called the attacks "partisan politics," while one Florida newspaper noted the damage legislators and the College Republican National Committee (CRNC) did to themselves when they disagreed with the work of PIRG: "That the CRNC has chosen to make PIRGs a partisan issue is not to their credit. Presumably, 'public interest' transcends party lines and is, in fact, the sole aim of government—preserving the public good."

Florida is not the only PIRG under attack from the College Republicans. In fact, the College Republican National Committee, in an effort unrelated to the Republican party (PIRGs have supporters from both political parties), has made PIRGs a target for defeat nationwide. The CRNC announced in a letter to members, "Our new anti-PIRG project is called 'The CRNC PIRG-Free Zone Project,' and we are rewarding certificates of recognition to all State CR Federations who rid their state of this pestilence. . . ."

Most students recognize these attacks are a measure of PIRG's effectiveness—if the group was not making an impact on social policy and consumer and environmental issues, no one would even notice it. So, though the attacks are likely to continue, so will the work of PIRGs. "Nowhere are the College Republicans or the Young Americans for Freedom a match for PIRGs," says Donald Ross, "because they can't match the student support PIRGs have."

# EIGHT

# PIRGs: The Future

One woman who was studying psychology in Colorado in 1976 recalls that she helped COPIRG that summer when it petitioned to qualify a ballot proposal requiring the return of beverage bottles. Though her work with COPIRG did not last long, ten years later, now out of law school, she remembers being involved with the group and she still keeps track of what the PIRG is doing in her home state.

A student in Indiana worked on utility issues for the PIRG during his years of college. Now he is an economist for the federal Office of Management and Budget.

These examples and others in the book point out the variety of opportunities PIRGs offer a diverse student body. Moreover, for every successful project described in the book there are many more that could be included; for every student who is named there are countless others who have been involved and are getting involved each day. And some of those will make a career of public interest work and others will pursue seemingly unrelated fields. Some will spend more time on PIRG projects than on class work; others will work with PIRG only a short time. Some will select a field of study because of exposure to new ideas through PIRG; others will learn through PIRG how public interest work combines with the field they have chosen already.

Whatever a student's involvement with a PIRG, new insights, new interests, new priorities, and new skills are sure to surface. Students are learning to use the system to bring about change. They have found, as PIRG lobbyists, researchers, and organizers, that the perception of students as a segment of society that does not yet have a role in decisionmaking is dissolving. What is taking its place is the realization among lawmakers, government officials, industry executives, and nonstudents that students can consistently and competently represent the public interest in any arena.

That is the kind of organization Ralph Nader had in mind when he first proposed the formation of PIRGs. In 1970, if you had asked Nader or any of the people trying to get PIRGs started where the movement would go in the future, they would have answered, "The sky's the limit!" They would have told you how students could do in-depth investigations and publish reports; how they could promote legislation that would curb pollution or encourage conservation; how students could, with the help of a staff attorney, pursue justice on consumer and environmental issues in the courts. All this and more.

But ask them how much influence students would have as lobbyists. Ask them how extensively the reports would be covered in the media. Ask them how important the court cases would be. They probably never would have told you that lobbyists for the PIRGs would see many of their bills become law each year, that PIRG reports would be distributed internationally, that PIRG members would testify before state legislatures and Congress, or that some PIRG court cases would go to the Supreme Court. People who were with PIRG in the early days often say they had no idea, really, how sophisticated and effective the PIRG movement would become.

Now, PIRG activists can more accurately predict the PIRG's future because they have seen its past. They have seen PIRGs start from scratch and grow into prominent consumer organizations making important changes in social policy; they have witnessed the range of issues students work on through PIRGs; they have seen thousands of students walk into PIRG offices with concern for an issue, and they have seen those students research, write, and speak before the public on the issues that interested them—all through the PIRG. Most activists were at one time those enthusiastic newcomers to the group themselves.

So, ask today's PIRG activist: "What is the future of the PIRG movement?"

"The sky's the limit!"

The phrase is bandied about often. It is a reminder of the idealism that is an ever-present component of PIRG work. Now, though, that statement is built around a proven framework for building the PIRGs and increasing student and community participation in the political process.

There are several reasons why the PIRG's place in the future is certain. First is its past success. Students and people in the community are familiar with the effectiveness the organization has had on important issues and will be supportive of continued PIRG work.

Second, the hundreds of students who came through PIRG while in college and have stayed in the movement are lending their considerable skills and historical perspective to PIRGs as staff members. Someone who lobbied in the legislature as a student will bring his or her knowledge of what worked and what did not work there to a position as legislative director, or the person who did a great deal of research on a particular topic can come on staff to head future projects on that issue. With growing expertise among PIRG staff, the skills and techniques that have made a PIRG effort effective in one state can be shared with other PIRGs.

Third, the network of support has expanded on campus and throughout society as PIRGs develop more sophisticated community programs such as the door-to-door Citizen Outreach Project.

Fourth, new PIRGs are being added to campuses each semester, even in states with small PIRGs or none until now.

It is a good thing PIRGs have grown in size and sophistication; the problems they tackle are more complex and their opponents are more determined. In 1970, not many people were aware of toxic chemicals such as dioxin and PCB. Now PIRGs in several states are leading the drive to protect drinking water and the environment from these and other hazardous wastes and to ensure proper cleanup of waste sites. New York PIRG, with eleven years' experience investigating the problem of toxics, writing reports, informing the public, and successfully advocating laws to provide for hazardous waste cleanup, is now lending its expertise to PIRGs in other states.

The Minnesota PIRG, with more than a dozen years of aggressive litigation, can offer assistance with legal issues. The Oregon and Missouri PIRGs have shared their experience in utility issues with other PIRGs. And the whole range of PIRG expertise is used by community groups concerned with everything from housing for the elderly to fair utility rates.

PIRGs have always sought strong ties to the community. The social change that students are working for will not spring solely from an active campus; people in the community must join the effort. As many of the projects profiled in this book show, legislators who may not have been impressed with student proposals took notice when the students presented thousands of signatures on petitions or when PIRGs sparked massive letter-writing campaigns. Demonstrated widespread support in the community is a vital ingredient to most PIRG efforts.

## PIRGs: The Future

Getting a person to write a letter helps promote one issue, but it also does something more: It helps that person recognize the worth of participating in the political process. Say a Massachusetts resident has written his or her state legislator a couple of times but never seen any results flow from the letter, except maybe a thank-you form letter. But then someone from MASSPIRG encourages that person to write in favor of the bottle bill, and a few months later it becomes law. That person, and the thousands of others who wrote, will see first hand how important it is to make their opinion known, and in particular to make it known in coordination with others so it will have the most impact.

Coordinating letter-writing campaigns is only a small part of the community organizing and educating PIRGs do. With all PIRG activities, it is important to provide the public with information, whether it is a survey of dangerous toys that have not been removed from the market, or a free workshop on home insulation. Press coverage allows people to find out about specific projects, but rather than rely on that, many PIRGs have developed door-to-door operations to explain PIRG projects in person and to gain support for the group with signatures on petitions and with contributions. Because of the canvass, PIRGs reach hundreds of thousands of supporters each year: Almost a million people signed on in support of PIRGs last year. Canvassing also builds a base of people who are informed about PIRG efforts and who can be mobilized quickly to voice their opinions when legislators prepare to vote or when regulatory agencies consider consumer petitions. The coalition between PIRGs and community groups serves both well: PIRG projects are more likely to be successful, and people in the community have the benefit of seeing their voice have a greater impact because it is joined with thousands of others.

PIRGs in eighteen states plus the District of Columbia

have ongoing canvasses. Again, the sharing of information and proven techniques allows those in one state to benefit from the experience of those in another state.

From what we have seen of PIRGs, it is clear that they will be as much a match for future problems as they have been for problems in the past. New challenges may be more complex than past ones, but students' sophistication in activism is also increasing.

The PIRG framework for student training is proven: Students can be effective in a variety of arenas with the help of professionals. Students do not have to confine their concern to campus-related issues; rather, they can have an impact on issues with statewide, national, and even international significance. Finally, learning-by-doing allows students to find out about their own interests and skills.

Students in the future will undoubtedly be facing some very different problems in society from those faced even a few years ago. But PIRGs can be just as effective then in addressing fundamental issues. The benefits and risks of new technology must be assessed, and during its development, natural resources and the safety of the public must be safeguarded. As computers begin providing access to more and more important services and information sources, the ability of all citizens to have access to those services and information will become an issue. And, as always, PIRGs will need to continue encouraging and providing the channels for citizen participation—whatever the issue.

Students getting involved with PIRGs today have the benefit of PIRGs' years of experience and established reputation in the community and the legislature as representatives of the public interest. Of course, the track record of the organizations will not continue to improve without new students each year to make the projects, investigations, reports, and lobbying efforts successful.

## PIRGs: The Future

After reading a book describing all the problems PIRGs tackle, it almost seems as if an invitation to join the group is an invitation to take on the weight of the world's troubles. But chances are, if you read the newspapers, watch the news, and have any plans to be around for the next fifty years or so, the weight of those problems is already with you. It makes sense to join with others in shouldering that weight. What working for PIRGs can do is bring together the creativity and energy of many people to provide community solutions for today and tomorrow.

# APPENDIX A

# How to Start a PIRG

Back in the fall and winter of 1970-71, students at public and private colleges and universities overcame apathy, cold, and reluctant administrators and trustees to form the nation's first PIRGs—OSPIRG in Oregon and MPIRG in Minnesota, both of which continue to operate today. Inspired by the success of these first PIRG organizing drives, students in Missouri, Vermont, Connecticut, Massachusetts, California, North Carolina, New Jersey, and New York launched their own PIRGs. Today, there are twenty-five state PIRGs already operating, with others in Canada and Australia, and more in the process of formation.

Over the years, certain organizing skills have been developed. Campaign literature, poster designs, and leaflets have been created. However, it is a testament to the skills of the first Minnesota and Oregon organizers that the very same formula for forming PIRGs that worked well in 1971 can be used today.

This section is a summary of what needs to be done on a campus to form a PIRG or a new PIRG chapter. First, you must inform the student body and faculty about PIRG. What is it? How does it work? What are its

*Appendix A. How to Start a PIRG*

achievements? How will it benefit and enrich the educational process? These and similar questions must be answered and the information must be disseminated to a large portion of the student body.

Then the student body must express support in a democratic manner for the proposal to create a PIRG chapter. This is done through a referendum, which is how students elect student government officers and decide other important campus questions; or a petition drive, which can also demonstrate majority support on campus for a PIRG.

The final step is to ensure that if the education campaign is successful and the petition drive or referendum wins student support, the PIRG is actually formed. To avoid difficulties in the last stages of organizing, PIRG organizers must make sure that the university administration and other student organizations are supportive from the outset.

Here is more detail about each of the steps in forming a PIRG. This section is intended only as an introduction to PIRG organizing. For more information and help in starting a PIRG, write to: Center for Study of Responsive Law, P.O. Box 19367, Washington, D.C. 20036. Please include your permanent address, your college address, your college year, and your major.

## A GUIDE FOR ORGANIZERS

### Step 1. Know about PIRG

Before you can reach out to the student body at large, you must thoroughly understand the student PIRG concept yourself. Reading this book is a good start; *Action for a Change*, by Ralph Nader and Donald Ross, is also a good way to learn the civic theory underlying the PIRG idea. You can also read a PIRG's annual reports, legislative programs, newsletters, publications lists, and news clippings to learn a great deal about the activities of the existing groups. A directory of PIRG addresses is in Appendix B, below. Reviewing PIRG bylaws will help you to understand their structure, the rights of member schools, and the roles of the student boards and staff. Finally, visiting a PIRG office and talking firsthand to students and staff is an excellent way to find out more. PIRG staff and students have tight schedules, though; be sure to arrange in advance to meet with them.

### Step 2. Know about the School

Know as much as possible about what you are trying to organize: Find out how many students are enrolled full-time, and what number live on or off campus. Get copies of campus bylaws and university rules covering the funding system for student activities, clubs, student government, and so on. Learn about the democratic procedure for funding new activities—by referendum, by petition, or both—and also learn who must approve new funding after an activity receives student support (sometimes it's the student government; other times, the university president; often, it's the board of trustees). Learn about the university president and trustees. Also find out the history of any past PIRG organizing efforts on campus, if there have been any. Try to locate potential allies—students or faculty who have worked with PIRGs in other states and progressive faculty members or school organizations.

### Step 3. Inform Others about PIRG

When an organizing core group of students is prepared, the process of informing the student body at large can begin. While each campus is different, there are some

*Appendix A. How to Start a PIRG*

proven methods for distributing information to the student body. Here are some of them:

- distributing leaflets describing PIRG
- putting up posters in well-trafficked areas
- setting up a table near the cafeteria to talk to students as they enter and exit
- writing up a series of articles and letters to the editor of the school paper
- appearing on the school radio station
- chalking blackboards in the morning before classes begin
- talking in classes for five or ten minutes
- going door to door in dormitories or attending floor or dorm meetings
- speaking in clubs and the student senate during their regular meetings.

Organizers of PIRGs in the past have also put on musical performances, painted billboards, sponsored movies, hung banners, and promoted other ideas to attract attention and convey their message. (For more on this, see "Some Words about Publicity," below.)

At the same time that your group is informing the student body at large, two or three members of the core group should be reaching out to student leaders, important members of the faculty, and administrators. This core should be very familiar with campus bylaws, the make-up of the student government, and other things about the campus listed in Step 2 above. Great effort must be made to ensure united student support.

### Step 4. Demonstrate Support for PIRG

Informing students about the merits of PIRG does not automatically mean that they will unilaterally expend time and effort to register their support. Rather than sitting back and letting students bear the burden of showing support, PIRG organizers should reach out to students, help motivate them, and ease the way for them to demonstrate their support.

Democratic student support for PIRG is demonstrated in one of three ways: a petition drive, a referendum, or a combination of the two. Each procedure has certain advantages and disadvantages for the organizers, and some experienced PIRG organizers favor one over the other.

Massive petitioning is grueling work, and can wear out and discourage the core group of students. Done well, though, it can be a very effective way to show that a majority of students support PIRG—and it can also be a good way to expose the student body to the PIRG idea, since it involves direct contact between the organizers and the students. Referenda, on the other hand, are the usual method for electing student governments and deciding on student activities, and since they are completed more quickly, running one successfully does not need to be as wearing as constant petitioning can be—saving organizers' energy for what can be the most difficult step in organizing a PIRG, Step 5 below.

Sometimes a petition drive is required before a referendum can be held, in which case the two methods are combined. The best way to determine which method to use at your campus will be by talking to other experienced PIRG organizers. The procedures for running petition drives or referenda also vary from school to school; under

*Appendix A. How to Start a PIRG*

Step 2, you will have learned what procedures exist for your particular campus.

All of the approaches listed under Step 3 to inform students about PIRG can be used and reinforced during election time or a petition drive. If the core organizing group begins with two or three students at the outset of the educational drive, by the time of the vote or petitioning it should number in the dozens. Many of the new recruits will be less highly motivated than the original core organizers. But they are critical to the success of the organizing drive and should be motivated and assigned key tasks at critical locations during the referendum or petition drive.

*Step 5. Getting Approval*

This is a crucial step. The best intentions and most concerted efforts on all the other steps can be wasted if insufficient effort is made on this step. Under Step 2 above, you will have discovered who must approve a student activity and funding, after support for it is demonstrated by the student body.

The effort to gain that approval is merely an extension of informing others about PIRG—only this time you will be focusing on student government members, the university president, and the board of trustees. Write to these people, meet with them, inform them about PIRG theory and activities, and enlist their support. Now is the time, too, to make use of contacts you will have made during previous education efforts, including sympathetic student government leaders, faculty, university officials, alumni, and community leaders—who should also write to the university president and board of trustees urging them to support PIRG.

## GUIDELINES FOR PIRG SPEAKERS AND PETITIONERS

1. Know the PIRG program inside and out. Read all materials thoroughly, including *Action for a Change*. If you have any doubts or questions, resolve them before attempting to speak or petition on behalf of the program.
2. Work with other PIRG people in small group sessions until you feel capable of making a strong presentation. Use role-playing techniques to expose any weaknesses and to sharpen your approach. Subject the whole program to close critical scrutiny.
3. Develop your own style and format. Don't try to memorize a set speech or to imitate someone else's approach. Vary your presentation enough to keep it spontaneous and fresh.
4. Anticipate objections, questions, and criticisms, and be able to respond to them effectively.
5. Avoid a defensive, apologetic stance. You're not asking people to do you any favors by signing the petition. You're asking them to join together for a better education and a better society.
6. In dealing with resistance, try to distinguish between genuine philosophical or practical objections on the one hand and convenient rationalization on the other. Make your counterarguments responsive to the individual's particular criticism or opposition.
7. Set realistic daily and weekly quotas for signatures, and then make every effort to meet them.

*Appendix A. How to Start a PIRG*

8. Talk specifics. People have difficulty relating to generalities. Read periodicals and papers to stay up on current local and national issues, and connect these issues to PIRG.

9. Avoid a hard sell. Most individuals will recognize the value of PIRG if the idea is intelligently presented to them. Don't collect signatures indiscriminately or attempt to railroad people into signing. Be sure the concept is clearly understood before soliciting a signature.

10. Be familiar with other PIRGs and what they have done. Cite specific examples. (This book is full of them.)

11. Be on the lookout for new recruits. Anyone who manifests some interest should be asked to work immediately on petitions, publicity, whatever.

12. Make it easy for people to get to you. The PIRG compaign should be highly visible and accessible. Everyone connected with the organizing effort should be readily identifiable; buttons, armbands, etc., are a help.

13. Demonstrate your conviction, but don't make extravagant, unrealistic claims. Students are justifiably skeptical about wild promises and catch-all instant solutions to complex social problems. Hence PIRG is probably best represented in terms of opportunity or potential.

## RECRUITING

### *Adopt the Organizer's Perspective*

Adopting the "organizer's perspective" means learning to view your campus in terms of the various segments of the campus community. What type of students go there? Where do they live—off campus, on campus, independently, in fraternity or sorority houses? What are the different academic departments? What clubs or organizations exist and what are their functions? How many students are full-time, part-time? Where do students congregate during the day, and at night? Which kinds of students at which places? Where do you and the other people interested in PIRG fit into these patterns?

Attracting students to PIRG is primarily a job of *communicating* the PIRG concept. For this reason, it is essential to break the campus down into its various segments, for some segments never come into touch with one another. You will probably find that organizing among those people you see regularly will be fairly easy. However, if you are an on-campus student and you find that all the people you work with are also on-campus students, it may be because on- and off-campus students do not communicate very often. If you are to involve these other students, conscious efforts must be made to reach them.

As an organizer, you want not only to inform but to recruit—you need *people* to get into PIRG and make it go. Experience has shown that it is helpful to look for two kinds of people: those with experience and contacts who have already proven themselves to be outstanding; and those with energy and potential yet untapped.

*Appendix A. How to Start a PIRG*

### *Perform a Talent Search*

On any campus, there will be certain people who share a deep concern for social problems, and have demonstrated this concern in many ways. There will also be people who may never have become involved in social issues, but have nevertheless demonstrated their abilities in scholastics, public speaking, human relations, and so on, and may very well "step into" public interest work once exposed to this opportunity. If these people are not already too wrapped up in other activities, then they are the people most likely to become involved in PIRG. As an organizer, your job is to discover who these people are. Begin by assuming you know absolutely no one on campus. You may otherwise overlook good people whom you should have known would be interested.

**Contact people.** Start with faculty members (beginning with the most obvious, such as political science, sociology, environmental sciences—but expanding to cover all departments, and all class levels); the student affairs office and counseling office; campus ministers; minority leaders; campus social action groups and other organizations; and any others who might know the campus well.

**Inform these people.** Explain the PIRG concept. Ask them for names of thoughtful, concerned, and talented students who might be interested in PIRG, and others who would be interested in helping organize a PIRG. Then send an introductory letter to all recommended students, in which you briefly explain PIRG, invite them to the first organizational meeting, and say you will be trying to contact them personally as well.

**Follow up.** Make personal phone calls and/or visits. Get commitments from interested students to come to the first organizational meeting. *Be sure to call them the night before the meeting to remind them of the time and place.*

### Conduct General Publicity

At the same time you are recruiting from a select group of students recommended to you, it is necessary to make a broad appeal as well to the entire student body. You should probably get initial media coverage of the PIRG concept and your first organizational meeting. Interest your student newspaper in an article and an interview, and get announcements on your campus and other radio stations. Put up signs around campus that tell a little of what PIRG is about, and announce prominently the first organizational meeting. Finally, put the announcement of the meeting in your campus announcements or calendar, if they exist.

## HOLDING THE ORGANIZATIONAL MEETING

What happens at the first meeting of your organizational group can in many ways affect the kind of PIRG drive you have. If you have done your job in raising interest in PIRG, there should be many people coming out of curiosity to find out exactly what a PIRG is. If this first meeting is deliberate and exciting for them, they are likely to return. Remember, they are not yet as convinced about PIRG as you are—put yourself in their position when planning this meeting.

*Appendix A. How to Start a PIRG*

Some general points to consider are:

- Know why you are meeting and what you want out of the meeting.
- Remember that meetings should be fun and spirited.
- Communicate the importance of what the group is doing. The point is to get something done, build interest and commitment, and inspire people to come back.

Here's a suggested procedure for the meeting:

**Start by making introductions.** It is always best to begin with introductions of your speakers. This is especially true for the first meeting of a group, but keep it brief. If the audience is small, ask each person's name.

**Discuss the PIRG concept.** Next up is an explanation of PIRG by someone who is knowledgable and fairly eloquent on the subject. The explanation should last no more than about fifteen minutes, with roughly equal emphasis on the concept and structure of PIRG, and what it has done and could be doing. If the presentation of the PIRG concept is done well, there should be numerous questions on how to proceed. Answer them as clearly and concisely as possible. Be sure to direct students to your written materials as well.

**Describe the job at hand.** Try to complete the discussion and move on to a talk on the job at hand: getting the support of the student body on petitions or in a referendum, and getting the approval of the college's board of trustees for PIRG funding. This talk should include a brief explanation of how this has been done at other schools, expressed in terms of setting goals and designing strategies to achieve these goals.

If the group at your meeting is large enough to break into task committees, do so. At the very least, get commitments from individuals to work on the following areas: communications and publicity; building support (getting endorsements from faculty, businesses, administrators, and politicians); and petitioning and public speaking.

***Wrap up.*** Participants should leave the meeting accepting specific assignments and deadlines. Enumerate these assignments when summarizing the meeting so that all participants know what is happening. If time permits and participants are willing, this might be good time to break into smaller groups to determine how to implement specific tasks. You should also provide refreshments for postmeeting socializing.

***Follow up.*** From this point on, schedule full meetings only when it is necessary to communicate or when they are needed to build momentum. Each committee should be expanded into a larger group performing its part of the organizing function. Call each small group or committee leader two or three days after your first meeting to make sure that things are moving. Check with each committee regularly and stress the urgency of meeting deadlines. Remember that communication among core group members is key.

## SOME WORDS ABOUT PUBLICITY

The primary job of PIRG organizers is to communicate the message of PIRG effectively to the student body. Though each campus is different—and therefore each publicity drive will be different—there are certain basic

*Appendix A. How to Start a PIRG*

principles to follow. The key to success is to get your message into the "grapevine"—to get people talking about your cause. For this to happen, your publicity must make an impression on people. Here's how:

- *Interest.* Your message must be of some personal interest to your audience.
- *Bigness.* Have your message "coming out of the walls" literally wherever people go (to study, to eat, to play, to church, to shop, etc.).
- *Novelty.* Combined with bigness, the use of novel methods of communication to catch people's attention should ensure success. Ideas include posters in odd places, multimedia displays, banners, bumper stickers, and buttons.
- *Neatness.* When dealing with the general public, it is always worthwhile to present a neat, professional look rather than a sloppy one. In attracting attention and establishing credibility, your message must stand out as different from others. Think of your own experience—what catches your eye? What do you find easy to look at and to read?
- *Consistency.* Observing a common theme or graphic design in your publicity drive will help people identify with your cause. A common phrase or logo in all publicity is a good idea.

## FOR MORE INFORMATION

To repeat, for more information and help in starting a PIRG, write to: Center for Study of Responsive Law, P.O. Box 19367, Washington, D.C. 20036. Please include your permanent address, your college address, your college year, and your major.

# APPENDIX B

# Directory of Public Interest Research Groups

**Alaska PIRG (AKPIRG)**
P.O. Box 1093
Anchorage, AK 99510
(907) 278-3661

**British Columbia PIRG (BCPIRG)**
Staff Collective
Simon Fraser University
Room TC-304-305
Barnaby, British Columbia
V51S6 CANADA
(604) 291-4360

**California PIRG (CALPIRG)**
1147 S. Robertson #202
Los Angeles, CA 90035

Berkeley, CA 94704
(415) 642-9952

**Colorado PIRG (COPIRG)**
1724 Gilpin Street
Denver, CO 80218
(303) 355-1861

**Connecticut PIRG (CONNPIRG)**
University of Connecticut
Box U-8
Storrs, CT 06268
(203) 486-5002

**Florida PIRG (FPIRG)**
1441 E. Fletcher Avenue
Tampa, FL 33612
(813) 971-7564

*Appendix B. Directory of Public Interest Research Groups*

**Indiana PIRG (INPIRG)**
Activities Desk
Indiana Memorial Union
Bloomington, IN 47405
(812) 335-7575

**Iowa PIRG (IPIRG)**
Iowa State University
Memorial Union, Room 36
Ames, IA 50011
(515) 294-8094

**Maine PIRG (USMPIRG)**
92 Bedford Street
Portland, ME 04103
(207) 780-4044

**Maryland PIRG (MARYPIRG)**
3110 Main Dining Hall
University of Maryland
College Park, MD 20742
(301) 454-5601

**Massachusetts PIRG (MASSPIRG)**
29 Temple Place
Boston, MA 02111
(617) 292-4800

**PIRG in Michigan (PIRGIM)**
Box 4375
Ann Arbor, MI 48109
(313) 662-6597

**Minnesota PIRG (MPIRG)**
2412 University Avenue SE
Minneapolis, MN 55414
(612) 376-7554

**Missouri PIRG (MOPIRG)**
4144 Lindell Boulevard
Suite 219
Saint Louis, MO 63108
(314) 534-7474

**Montana PIRG (MONTPIRG)**
356 Corbin Hall
Missoula, MT 59812
(406) 243-2907

**New Jersey PIRG (NJPIRG)**
84 Paterson Street
New Brunswick, NJ 08901
(201) 247-4606

**New Mexico PIRG (NMPIRG)**
University of New Mexico
Box 66 SUB
Albuquerque, NM 87131
(505) 277-2757

**New York PIRG (NYPIRG)**
9 Murray Street
New York, NY 10007
(212) 349-6460

**Ohio PIRG (OPIRG)**
Wilder Box 25
Oberlin, OH 44074
(216) 775-8137

**Ontario PIRG (ONPIRG)**
229 College Street
Room 203
Toronto, Ontario M5T1R4
CANADA
(416) 598-1576

**Oregon Student PIRG (OSPIRG)**
027 SW Arthur
Portland, OR 97201
(503) 222-9641

**Rhode Island PIRG (RIPIRG)**
228 Weybosset Street
Fourth Floor
Providence, RI 02903
(401) 331-7474

**United States PIRG (U.S. PIRG)**
215 Pennsylvania Avenue, S.E.
Washington, DC 20003
(202) 546-9707

**Vermont PIRG (VPIRG)**
43 State Street
Montpelier, VT 05602
(802) 223-5221

**Virginia PIRG (VAPIRG)**
Student Activities Office
College of William and Mary
Campus Center, Room 203
Williamsburg, VA 23185
(804) 235-4557

**Washington PIRG (WASHPIRG)**
5628 University Way NE
Seattle, WA 98105
(206) 526-8843

**West Virginia PIRG (WVPIRG)**
Mountainlair, SOW
West Virginia University
Morgantown, WV 26506
(304) 293-2108

PIRGs are in the process of formation in Georgia, Illinois, North Carolina, Pennsylvania, Texas and Wisconsin. For more information write to: "New PIRGs," Center for Study of Responsive Law, P.O. Box 19367, Washington, DC 20036.

# Index

Academic credit, 177–79
Acid Rain Caravan, xx, 105–7
*Action for a Change* (Nader and Ross), xii, 11, 79, 201–2, 206
Activists, xvi, 34; *see also* Student activists
Advocacy, xvi, xvii, xviii, xxv, 6, 29, 88, 177, 179, 180–81
AFL-CIO, 13, 185
*Agenda for Citizen Involvement* (newsletter), 78, 181
Ahmed, Karim, xiii, 171–75
Alaska PIRG (AKPIRG), 179
*Albany Times Union*, 89
Alsop, Judge, 26
American University PIRG, 145
Anderson, Jack, 9, 16
Anderson, Marion, 16
Anderson, Warren, 63, 64
Antinuclear movement, xxiii, 150, 161; *see also* Nuclear issues
Antiwar movement, xxiii, 144–45, 166; *see also* Vietnam War
Apartment Owners Association (Colo.), 121, 123
Armstrong, William, 128
Arnott, Robert, 116
Artist, Bill, 122
Asbestos, 13, 173

Asbestosis, 84
AT&T, 37
Atomic Energy Act, 31
Atomic Energy Commission, 113
Auto industry, 3–4
Auto repair, xi, xviii, xxii, 12, 87
Auto safety, 3–4

Babcock/Wilcox (co.), 161
Bank on Brooklyn (BOB), 102–4
Banks, banking, xxi, 173; check clearing time, xx, 37, 87; Cleveland, Ohio, 160, 163–64; redlining, 99–104
Bauer, William, 54, 55, 56, 57, 58, 59
Beverage industry, 40, 41, 42, 43; *see also* Bottle bills
Birmingham, Susan, 132
Bloustein, Edward J., 189
Bottle bills, 84, 113–14, 135; Massachusetts, xix, 39–45
Boston College, Pulse Program, 178
Boundary Waters Canoe Area (BWCA) (Minn.), 22–24
British Columbia PIRG, 20
Bronx Legal Services, 143
Brooklyn College NYPIRG, 99–100
Brotman, Stanley, 189

217

Brown Lung Association (BLA), 48, 50, 53, 187
Brown lung disease, 20, 46–53
Brown University, 68
Burford, Anne Gorsuch, 116
Burgess, Rob, 17
*Burning Question, The* (report), 85
Burstein, Karen, 87–89, 185–86
Butts, Charles, 161
Byssinosis (brown lung disease), 20, 46–53

California, 31, 74; CUB, 34; Public Utility Commission, 86
California PIRG (CALPIRG), xix, 33, 66, 134, 200; and meat scandal, xx, 53–59
Campaign for Safe Energy (CSE), 133, 150–52
Carey, Hugh, 65, 140
Carson, Rachel: *Silent Spring*, 2
Carter, James, xxi, 52, 133, 151
Carter administration, 53
Cary, Steve, 63
*Caution: NCOSHA Is Dangerous to Your Health* (report), 51
*CBS News*, 179
Center for Study of Responsive Law, 4–5
Central Maine Power Company, 18
Central New York PIRG, 78
Check-clearing time, xx, 37, 87
Chemical pollution, 19–20, 90–99
Children's sleepwear, 112–13
Chiles, Lawton, 56
Chlopak, Bob, xiii, 144–52, 180
Citizen involvement in political process, xvi, xxv, xxvii–xxviii, 5, 18, 33, 67–69, 99–104, 152, 185, 198
Citizen Outreach Project (MASSPIRG), 133, 135, 196
Citizens Alliance, 187
Citizens' utility boards (CUBs), xxviii, 34–35, 86, 185
Citizenship, xxvi, 177, 183
City University of New York, 80

Civil Rights Act (1964), 2
Civil rights movement, xv–xvi, xxiii, xxiv–xxv, 2, 166, 171
Clean Air Act, 105, 128
Clean Water Act (CWA), 92, 93
Clean water lawsuits, 135
Cleveland, Ohio, 159, 160, 162–66
Cleveland Electric Illuminating Company (CEI), 163
Cleveland Trust Company, 160, 163–64
Coalition building, 185–87
College Republican National Committee (CRNC), 190, 191–92
College Republicans, 68, 124, 125–26, 127, 190–92
*Colorado Outlook* (newsletter), 129, 181
Colorado PIRG (COPIRG), 110–30, 193; newsletter: *Colorado Outlook*, 129, 181; organization of, 110–15
Colorado State University, 113, 115, 126
Commission on Financing Higher Education, 61
Commoner, Barry, 150
Community education, 39, 48, 50
Community organizing, xviii–xix, 39, 104, 197; *see also* Grass-roots organizing
Community support, 187, 196–97
Complaint centers, 182
Congress Watch, 156–57, 159
Connecticut, 43; Consumer Protection Department, 73
Connecticut PIRG (CONNPIRG), 69–74, 182–83, 200
Consumer guides, 181–82
Consumer protection, xvi, xxi, xxvii–xxviii, 5, 20–21, 58–59, 128; NYPIRG, 82, 87–88
Consumers Union, 174
Coro Foundation Fellowship, 169–70
"Corporate State, The" (Kurtz-Phelan), 110–11
Cronkite, Walter, 179

## Index

CUB. *See* Citizens' Utility Boards (CUBs)
Cuomo, Mario, 34, 85, 98, 140
Cutts, Royal B., 30

Davis, Josh, 17
Dayton, Chuck, 172–73
D.C. Power, 147, 148
DeFilippo, Frank, 126, 127
Democratic society, xxviii, xxix, 31, 126–27; *see also* Political process
Dental health, xx, 16–17
Denver Community College, 112
Discrimination, xv, 2, 113
Domurad, Frank, 107
Door-to-door canvassing, xix, 41, 42–43, 69, 85, 97, 129, 197–98
Draft registration, 25–26
Dukakis, Michael, 41
Dunne, John R., 97–98
Du Pont family, 111

Eastern Oregon State, 8
Ecology, 136, 172
Education, xvi, 28–29, 72, 176–177
Educational Testing Service (ETS), 60–67, 150, 182
Elderly (the), xviii, 88, 138, 185
Emergency Mobilization for the Right to Vote, 69
*Empty Pork Barrel, The* (report), 15–16
Energy issues, policy, xvi, xx, xxii, 133, 147, 151
Environmental Defense Fund (EDF), 91, 94
Environmental impact statements (EIS), 23
Environmental issues, xii, xiii, xvi, 32, 90–91, 115–19, 169, 171, 186
Environmental laws, 84–85
Environmental Protection Agency (EPA), 19–20, 35–36, 92, 113, 117; National Priority List, 119
Environmental rights act (Minn.), 22

Equal Justice Foundation (EJF), 158
Ezzard, Martha, 122

*Fallout on the Freeway* (report), 15
Federal Community Reinvestment Act, 103
Federal Trade Commission, 141; Consumer Protection Bureau, 143
Federal Water Pollution Control Act of 1972, 19
Ferguson, Karen, 156
Fields, David, 80
Financial aid for higher education, xx, 25–26, 128
Fisher, Helen, 153, 157
Fisher, Marjy, 152–59
Flanagan, John J., 62
Flatbush Federal Savings and Loan, 102
Florida: CUB, 34; PIRG, 191
Fonda, Jane, 165
Food and Drug Administration, 13
Forbes, George, 160
Ford Motor Company, 24
Freedom-of-information act(s) (FOIA), 83, 181–82
Friends of the Boundary Waters Wilderness, 24
Friends of the Earth, 148; Political Action Committee, xiii
Frizzell, Jon, 111
Funding (PIRGs), 9–10, 11, 80, 113–14, 124–26, 129, 134, 135, 145–46, 150, 154–55, 202; attacks on, 188–92
Funeral industry, 31–32, 187

Galda, Joseph, 189
*Galda* v. *Bloustein*, 189
Gardner, John, 101
General Motors, 3–4, 24, 71
Generic drug laws, 32, 83
George Washington University, 144, 148; National Law Center, 157–58; PIRG, 145–48
Georgetown University, 149; PIRG, 145–48

Gilbert, Pamela, 37
Gomberg, Marsha, 166–71
Grass-roots organizing, xix, 71–72, 82, 101, 104, 184–85
Green, Bill, 151
Green, Mark, 152; *Who Runs Congress?*, 151
Guenther, George, 51
Gulley, Wib, 48

Halfon, Jay, 83, 85–86, 87, 88
Hampshire College, 39, 131, 132
Handbooks, 129, 180, 182
Hands Across America, 184–85
Hands-on experience. *See* Learning by doing
Haney, Walter, 63
Hang, Walter, 91–96, 99
Hanley, Ed, 62, 64, 67
Harris, Robert, 91, 92
Hart, Gary, 128
Harvard University, 26
Hazardous Waste Cleanup Initiative (Mass.), xix–xx
"Hazardous Waste in Our Drinking Water" (report), xix–xx
Hazardous waste management, 15, 31, 32, 33, 35–36, 76, 84, 86, 96, 113, 196; COPIRG, 115–19; New York, 84, 90–99
*Hear Ye, Hear Ye!* (report), 137
Hearing aid sales practices, xii–xiii, 31–32, 83, 88, 137–42, 143, 185
Hershenson, Jay, 78, 79
Highland, Joseph, 91
Hind, Rick, 36
Hoffman, Allan, 30
Hogya, Frank, 54–55
Hooker Chemical (co.), 95, 96, 116
*Hopelessly Hoping* (report), 17
Hotlines, xviii, xxi, 128, 182–83
"How to Complain About Anything" (report), 129
Hudson River, 93

Idealism, xvi, xxi, xxiii, xxiv, 195
Illinois: CUB, 34

Indiana PIRG (INPIRG), xx, 152, 153–55, 157, 159
Industrial Chemical Survey(s) (New York), 86
Institute for Southern Studies, 50
Insurance redlining, 99, 103
Iowa PIRG, 182; Consumer Protection Service, 183
Issues, xi–xii, xvi, 5–6, 29, 32, 38, 169–70, 173, 191, 198
Izaak Walton League, 185

James, Franklin, 123

Karpinski, Gene, 33–34
Keeley, Dick, 178
Kennedy, Edward, 143
King, Edward, 42, 43
King, Martin Luther, Jr., 152–53, 171
"Know Your Rights" guides, 182
Kramer, Nancy, 81, 83, 142
Kucinich, Dennis, 160, 163, 164
Kurtz-Phelan, James, 112; "Corporate State, The," 110–11

Landlords, 120–23, 146, 147, 183–84, 187–88
Lange, Tim, 125, 130
LaValle, Kenneth, 62, 63, 64
Lawsuits, 26–27
Lawyers (PIRGs), 20–28, 68, 77
LEADS Program (Legal Education and Assistance in Defense of Students), 68
Learning by doing, xvii, 45, 67, 88, 143, 176–77, 179–80, 198
League of Women Voters, 158
Legal rights, 182, 196
Legislation, xii, xviii, 39, 58, 169, 194; NYPIRG-assisted, 83–89, 97–98; Vermont, 16–17
Lemon laws, xiii–xiv, 24, 69–74
Letter-writing campaigns, xviii–xix, 64, 196–97
Lewis and Clark College, 167, 169
Litigation programs, 21–28

## Index

Litwak, Mark, 78, 79, 81
Lloyd, Ed, 19, 20
Lobbying, xii, xvi, xviii, 28–32, 39, 48, 131, 132, 194; Connecticut lemon law, 72; hearing-aid sales bill, 138–42; NYPIRG, 82–89; truth-in-testing law, 63–64, 65
Lobbyists, industry, 85–86, 139–40
Lobbyists' registration law (New York), 83, 85, 87
Long Island, 95–97
Long Range Transport of Air Pollutants treaty, 105–6
Loretto Heights College, 112
Love Canal, 90, 116
Lubber, Mindy, 40–41, 42, 43–44, 45
Lumsden, John, 52

Macalester College, 26
McCarthy, Steven, 187
McClintock, Ruth, 28
McGlynn, John, 41–42
McGovern, George, 111, 160
McLean-Austen, Mary-Ann, 62, 66
Madden, Sister Loretta Anne, 120–21, 122
Magnusson-Moss Warranty Act, 73
Maine, 43; PIRG, 17–18
Marijuana decriminalization act (New York), 83
Markey, Edward, 133
Martin, David O'B., 106
Maryland PIRG, 181, 183
Massachusetts, 31, 74; bottle bill, 39–45; CUB, 34; Public Works Department, 45
Massachusetts Food Association, 44
Massachusetts PIRG (MASSPIRG), xix–xx, 78, 131, 132–33, 178, 197, 200; bottle bill campaign, xix, 40–45; Campaign for Safe Energy (CSE), 150–52
Massachusetts Soft Drink Association, 41
Meat industry, xx, 55–56, 57, 59
Meat scandal (Calif.), 53–59

Media, xvi, xviii, xxiv, 15, 16, 17, 18; use of, experience in, 56–57, 59, 72
Media coverage, 113, 194; *see also* Press coverage
Medical guides, 181
Meirzwinski, Ed, 70, 71–72
Merchant, James A., 48, 50, 52–53
Metropolitan State College (Denver), 112
Metzenbaum, Howard, 156
Meyer, Chris, 84
Mica, Dan, 157
Michael, Philip, 107–8
Michigan PIRG (PIRGIM), 15–16, 27, 181
Michigan Public Service Commission, 27
Mid-Atlantic Legal Foundation (MALF), 134, 188–90
Miller, Carl, 127
Miller, James, 26–27
Minneapolis Police Department, 22
Minnesota Civil Liberties Union, 26
*Minnesota Daily, The* (newspaper), 26
Minnesota PIRG (MPIRG), xiii, xx, 11, 12, 13, 20, 32, 172–74, 175, 182, 185, 196, 200; litigation program, 21–27; newsletter: *StateWatch*, 181
Minnesota Senior Citizens Association, 185
Minnesota Trial Lawyers, 185
Minorities, 67, 107
Missouri PIRG (MOPIRG), xx, 27–28, 176, 182, 185, 196, 200; newsletter: *MOPIRG Reports*, 181
MIT, 26
Moogan, Diane, 103–4
Moogan, Tom, 103–4
Moore, Thad, 47, 48, 50
Moorman, Ann, 115, 127
Moorman, Tim, 115
*MOPIRG Reports* (newsletter), 181
Morrano, Michael, 73
Moscovitz, Paul, 93
Motl, Jon, 114–15
Moynihan, Daniel P., 3

Municipal Light System (Muny) (Cleveland, Ohio), 163–64
Murphy, Joseph, 80, 177

Nader, Ralph, xi, 9, 61, 75, 78, 135, 136, 150, 172, 179, 194; Citizen Action Group, 110; Congress Watch, 156–57; and establishment of PIRGs, 3–5, 6–7; "Reign of ETS, The," 60; and Donald Ross: *Action for a Change*, xii, 11, 79, 201–2, 206; *Unsafe at Any Speed*, 3
Nader's Raiders, 4, 5, 151
Nairn, Allan, 61, 62, 63–64, 65
National Environmental Policy Act (NEPA), 22–24
National Institute of Safety and Health (NOSH), 51
National PIRG, xxi, 149–50
National Pollutant Discharge Elimination System (NPDES), 19
National Science Foundation, 169
National Student Campaign Against Hunger, 184–85
National Student Campaign for Voter Registration (NSCVR), 68–69
Natural Resources Defense Council (NRDC), xiii, 174–75
Neuman, Sharon, 177
New Jersey PIRG (NJPIRG), xx, xxi, 10, 18–20, 66, 134–35, 200; attacks on, 188–89, 190
New Mexico PIRG, xix, 181
New York City, 107–8
New York PIRG (NYPIRG), xiii, xix, xx, 32, 75–109, 200; Citizens Alliance, 187; coalition building, 185, 186; Fuel Buyers Group, 76; lawsuit against, 189–90; Legislative Internship Program, xii, 78, 88, 136–37, 141; newsletter: *Agenda for Citizen Involvement*, 78, 181; organization, size of, 77–80; publications, 78, 181, 182; J. Siegel and, 136–44; strength of, 89; and toxic wastes, xx–xxi, 196; Toxics Project, 85; and truth in testing, xx, 60–61, 62–67

New York Public Service Commission, 34
New York (state), 74; Atomic Energy Commission, 83; CUB, 34; Energy Research and Development Authority, 83; Public Service Commission, 86; truth-in-testing law, 60–61, 62–67
New York State Legislature: member profiles, 80–82, 136, 138
*New York Times*, 37, 65, 94
Niagara River, 95–97
North Carolina Department of Labor, 50–51
North Carolina PIRG (NCPIRG), 20, 46, 47–48, 49–52, 53, 181, 185, 187, 200
Northern States Power Co., 185
*Nothing to Smile About* (report), 16–17
Novick, Tom, 35
Nuclear Accountability Campaign, 36
Nuclear issues, 132, 133, 150–51, 161
Nuclear power industry, xii, 17–18, 29–31, 36–37
Nuclear Regulatory Commission, 17, 113
Nursing homes, 168–69

Oberlin PIRG, 161–62
Occupational health and safety, 13, 20, 187
Occupational Safety and Health Administration (OSHA), 46–47, 51, 52, 53; North Carolina, 47–48, 50–51
Ohio PIRG, 181
Ondrasik, Marilyn, 81, 101–2, 103, 104
1000 Friends of Oregon, 186–87
Ontario PIRG, xx, 20, 105–7, 181–82
Open-meetings law (New York), 83
Oregon: bottle bill, 40; CUB, 34–35
Oregon College of Education, 8
Oregon Student Public Interest Research Group (OSPIRG), 7–8, 11, 12, 34–35, 167–69, 170, 171, 185–87, 196, 200

# Index

Organizing, xvi, xxi, 72, 177; of PIRGs, 201–5, 206–7
Outreach programs, xix, 41, 155
"Overcoming the Obstacles" (manual), 68

*Pacific Gas & Electric v. California Public Utility Commission*, 35
Passannante, William, 139, 140, 142, 189
Pearson, C. B., 115, 185
Pension Rights Center, 156
PEPCO, 147–48, 149
Phelps, Doug, 45
Pike, Lewis, 63, 65–66
PIRGs. *See* Public Interest Research Groups (PIRGs)
Plain language bill (New York), 83
"Police badge" case (Minn.), 22
Political process, 152, 195, 197; *see also* Citizen involvement in political process; Learning by doing
Political reform, xvi; NYPIRG, 83–84, 87, 89
Political system: participation in, 179–80; *see also* Citizen involvement in political process
Pollution, xx, 5; *see also* Environmental issues; Water safety issue
Pomerance, Lenore, 148
Poudre River preservation, 128
Poundstone, Freda, 121
Presidential campaigns/elections, 67, 69, 133, 150–51, 152
Press conferences, 67, 94, 107, 140, 142
Press coverage, 41, 55, 63, 65, 67, 72–73, 94, 113, 197
Price-Anderson Act, 36–37
Price fixing, xxi, 56, 57–58, 59
*Prime Rip* (Schultz and Swanson), 59
Pritchard, Evan, 88
Problems, complex, xxi–xxii, 196, 198; *see also* Issues
Product liability, xviii, 155
Product safety, 32; *see also* Auto safety; Toy safety

Professional staff (PIRGs), xi, xix, 1, 7, 9, 11–12; scientists, 77, 171–75
Projects (PIRGs), xvii–xviii, 39–74, 150, 176, 180, 193, 196; choice of, 12; COPIRG, 111–30; NYPIRG, 80–81; researching, 14; watchdog, 18–20
Property tax reform, xviii, 32, 107–8
Public Citizen (organization), 5
Public citizens: student activists as, 6, 131–75
Public Counsel, 27
Public interest, xvi, 198; represented by students, 193–94
Public interest law, 157–58
Public Interest Research Groups (PIRGs), xi–xiv, xvi–xviii, xxi, 168; accomplishments, xix–xxi; in action: case histories, 39–74; in action: Colorado PIRG, 110–31; in action: New York PIRG, 75–109; action and reaction, 176–92; attacks on, 188–92; benefits to students, xii–xiii, xxvi, 45, 67, 88, 176–77, 179–80, 193–94, 198–99; bylaws, 202; campus, xxvi, 6–10; concept, 201, 211; directory of, 214–16; effectiveness of, 194, 195; future of, 193–99; how to start, 200–13; informing others about, 202–3, 205; literature of, 180–82; origin of, 1–13; recruiting for, 208–10; shared expertise, 195–96, 198; skills learned in, 179; staff, 195 (*see also* Professional staff [PIRGs]); state, 149, 150; structure and organization of, xvii, 1, 11–12, 210–12; support for, 204–5; value of, 152, 178
Public interest work, 131–35, 180, 193
Public opinion, xvi, 178
Public Utilities Commission, 147
Publications (PIRGs), 180–81, 202
Publicity, xviii, 55, 210, 212–13

Queens College, 80, 137, 138

223

Rather, Dan, 57, 59
*Ravaged River, The* (report), 95–97
Reagan, Patrick, 20
Reagan, Ronald, 151
Reagan administration, 52, 134
Redlining, 99–104, 105
Regis College, 112
"Reign of ETS, The" (Nader), 60
Rent control, 146–47
Rental agency reform law (Colo.), 111–12
Renter's rights (Colo.), 119–23
Reports (PIRGs), xxi, 15–18, 169, 194; NYPIRG, 75, 76, 77, 85, 92, 94–98, 100
Research, xvi, xviii, 14–38, 39, 177; and lobbying, 29
Retirement income reform, 156
Rhode Island PIRG (RIPIRG), 131–32, 133–34
Ribicoff, Abraham, 3
Richmond, Henry, 186–87
Right (the): challenges to COPIRG, 123–28, 134
Right-to-know laws, 86, 98, 135, 164–65
Roche, James, 4
*Rocky Mountain News*, 126
Rokakis, Jim, 159–66
Ross, Donald, xiii, 5, 6, 7, 8, 11–12, 28–29, 62, 143, 145, 156, 168, 172, 192; and NYPIRG, 78, 80–81, 82, 137, 139, 140, 142; Ralph Nader and: *Action for a Change*, xii, 11, 79, 201–2, 206
Russianoff, Gene, 107–8
Rutgers University, 10, 134, 188–89
Ryan, Tom, 29, 176

Saeks, Allan, 21, 172, 173
Safe Drinking Water Act, 36, 92
St. Jerome's Community Action Committee, 104
Schaffer, Dave, 89
Schaffer, Jesse, 108–9
Schroeder, Pat, 111

Schultz, George, 54–57, 58, 59; and Wayne Swanson, *Prime Rip*, 59
Segal, Milt, 44
Seibel, Megan, 127
Siegel, Jill, xii, xiii, 135–44
Siegel, Mike, 140–41
Sieroty, Alan, 169
Sierra Club, 185
Silberman, Jay, 93
*Silent Spring* (Carson), 2
Silkwood, Karen, 31
Simon, Loretta, 109
*60 Minutes*, xx, xxi, 57, 96–97
Small claims court, xviii, xxi, 83, 181
Smith, William P., 148
Social change, xxviii–xxix, 2, 135, 194, 196; lobbying for, 28–32
Social justice issue, xvi, 158, 194
Social problems, xvi, 2; *see also* Problems, complex
Social reform, xvi–xvii, xxiii, xxvii
Solomon, Steve, 66
Solomon amendment, 25–26
Souwaine, Jon, 132
Sowinski, Joan, 118
Special interests, xvi, 31–32, 33; lobbyists for, 86
Spock, Benjamin, 165
Spock, Mike, 48
State University of New York (SUNY), 10, 189–90; at Buffalo, 78–79, 80, 142
State utilities commissions, 27–28
*StateWatch* (newsletter), 181
Statute of limitations (New York), 76–77, 84–85
Straphangers Campaign (New York City), 76
Streamwalkers project, xx, 19–20
Stringer, Curt, 127
Student activism, xi–xii, xv, 2, 6, 166, 171, 198
Student activists: profiles of, 131–75
Student Mobilization Committee, 144
Students, xxi, xxiii–xxiv, 1, 5–6; and beginning of campus PIRGs, 6–10;

# Index

benefits to, from PIRG activity, xii–xiii, xvii, 29, 45, 67, 88, 176–77, 179–80, 193–94, 198–99; and bottle bill (Mass.), 39–45; as citizens, xvii, xxv–xxvi, 179–80; as class, xxii–xxiii, xxiv, 194; as "ideal activists," 135–36; power of, xv–xvi, xxiii
Suchman, E. Gail, 25, 26
Superfund (federal), 35–36, 119
Superfund bill (New York), 97–98, 99
Superfund law (Colo.), 119
Surveys (PIRGs), 14, 15–18
Swanson, Wayne, and George Schultz: *Prime Rip*, 59
Swarthmore College, 26
Swisher, Randy, 149
Syracuse University, 78–79, 80

*Take the Money and Run* (report), 100
Talbot, Annette, 121, 122–23
Tenant rights, 22, 119–23, 173, 182, 183–84, 188
*Testing for Toxics* (report), 36
Testing industry, 46, 53, 61, 66; *see also* Truth in testing
Textile industry, 46–53
Textile Workers Union of America, 47, 51–52
Three Mile Island, 150, 161
Timber sales from federal lands (Minn.), 22–24
Times Beach, Missouri, 90
Tobin, Tom, 35
Toward Utility Rate Normalization (TURN), 35
Toxic chemicals, wastes, xi, xx–xxi, 2, 84, 90–99, 196; *see also* Hazardous waste management
Toxics Victims Access to Justice campaign, 84–85
Toy safety, xii, 13, 113, 173
Triplett, Stephanie, 183–84
*Troubled Waters* (report), 94–95
Truth in testing, xx, 59–67, 84, 150

Union Electric (UE), 27–28
University of Colorado, Board of Regents, 110, 114, 125, 127, 130
University of Colorado in Boulder, 112, 114, 124–25
University of Denver, 111
University of Indiana, Living Learning Center (LLC), 153–54
University of Minnesota, 8, 26; PIRG, 171, 172–73
University of Northern Colorado, 112, 114
University of Oregon, 6–8
*Unsafe at Any Speed* (Nader), 3
Urban, Steve, 45
U.S. Forest Service, 23
U.S. Public Interest Research Group (U.S. PIRG), 32–38, 150
U.S. Supreme Court, 10, 25, 26, 31, 35, 52, 57–58, 86, 134, 189
USA for Africa, 184
Utility issues, 27–28, 33, 34, 86, 88, 113–14, 147–48, 187, 196

Vermont, 43; PIRG, xx, 16–17, 29–31, 32, 200
Vietnam War, xv, 2, 132, 160, 172
Volunteers in Service to America (VISTA) grants, 134, 149–50
"Voter Bill of Rights," 33–34
Voter registration, 2, 33–34, 67–69, 128

Wallace, Mike, 96–97
Ward, Kenneth, 131–35
Warrant of habitability law (Colo.), 120, 121, 122, 123
Washington, D.C., PIRG (DCPIRG), 146–48, 149, 152
Watchdog projects, 18–20
Water safety issue, xi, xix–xx, 19–20, 36, 91, 92, 93, 95–96, 98, 135, 196
Wathen, Thomas, 78, 125, 129–30, 188–89
Watt, James G., 115
Weinert, Kirk, 69

225

Weir, Brock, 160
Welch, Jim, 5, 6, 7
Welch, Kathleen, 36–37
West Valley nuclear reprocessing plant, 83–84
Western New York PIRG (WNY-PIRG), 79
*Who Runs Congress?* (Green), 151
Wild and Scenic Rivers Act, 128
Wilderness areas, 169

Wilson, Geoff, 117, 118
Wisconsin, xxviii; CUB, 34
WNET, 171
Woodcock, John J., 70–71, 72, 73
*Workers' Guide to Health and Safety*, 20
Wright, Lacy L., 49, 50
Writing, 39, 177

Young Americans for Freedom (YAF), 79, 190, 192